The Advanced Numeracy Test Workbook

Review key quantitative operations and practise for accounting and business tests

2nd edition

Mike Bryon

KoganPage

LONDON PHILADELPHIA NEW DELHI

First published in Great Britain and the United States in 2004 by Kogan Page Limited
Second edition, 2010
This edition, 2011

120 Pentonville Road	1518 Walnut Street, Suite 1100	4737/23 Ansari Road
London N1 9JN	Philadelphia PA 19102	Daryaganj
United Kingdom	USA	New Delhi 110002
www.koganpage.com		India

© Mike Bryon, 2004, 2010, 2011

The right of Mike Bryon to be identified as the author of this work has been asserted by him in accordance with the Copyright, Designs and Patents Act 1988.

ISBN   978 0 7494 6226 0
E-ISBN   978 0 7494 6227 7

British Library Cataloguing-in-Publication Data

A CIP record for this book is available from the British Library.

Library of Congress Cataloging-in-Publication Data

Bryon, Mike.
    The advanced numeracy test workbook : review key quantitative operations and practise for accounting and business tests / Mike Bryon. – 2nd ed.
        p. cm.
    ISBN 978-0-7494-6226-0 – ISBN 978-0-7494-6227-7 (ebook)   1. Numeracy–Problems, exercises, etc.
2. Reasoning (Psychology)–Testing.   3. Employment tests.   4. Psychometrics.   I. Title.
    QA141.B73 2011
    513–dc22
                                                                                                          2010051627

Typeset by Graphicraft Ltd, Hong Kong
Printed and bound in India by Replika Press Pvt Ltd

Contents

Acknowledgements

I owe thanks to Jon Stephenson and Ed Hateley for contributing some practice questions for Tests 6 and 7. I dedicate this book to my wife Lola.

How to make best use of this book

Use this book to prepare for psychometric tests of your advanced numerical skills. It contains material suitable for extensively used assessments including ABLE Financial Appraisal, GMAT, SHL Graduate Battery and McKinsey Problem Solving tests.

These tests are widely used to select between candidates for management and graduate jobs and places on postgraduate courses. They comprise a standardized series of problems, either multiple choice or short answer, taken either with pen and paper, online or at a computer terminal. Strict time limits apply. At the advanced end of the testing spectrum they are likely to comprise a series or battery of sub-tests sat one after the other. They are likely to take a number of hours and be a major test of endurance. You will have to work quickly and very hard.

Users of this book are likely to face a psychometric test when they apply for a job or course of study. In this context psychometric tests are used for selective purposes and represent major competitions. You may well be competing against thousands of other candidates for a handful of positions. To succeed, you will have to take this challenge very seriously.

Everyone can improve his or her test score with practice. Even the numerically accomplished through practice will ensure that they maximize their advantage. Candidates who have not used their numerical skills for some years will need to relearn the rules and regain their lost speed and accuracy. Those who never got on with maths or science at school or university may need to commit many weeks of effort to mastering the skills they previously managed without.

Start your programme of practice by doing Test 1; then score yourself and use the interpretation of your score in the final chapter to determine the amount and type of practice you should undertake. Make sure that you start practising in good time. It is likely that you should practise for a minimum of 12 hours and perhaps as much as two hours a day for many weeks.

Be sure that you practise on material that is similar to that in a real test. It is essential that you establish the type of question contained in the real tests and restrict your practice to questions that are similar or the same as those that you face. The organization that has invited you to sit the test should provide you with detail of the type of question either as a booklet or on a website. Use this information to identify suitable practice material.

The limiting factor in terms of how much improvement can be realized through practice is often the amount of realistic material that is available on which to work. This book is intended to complement the existing Kogan Page book *How to Pass Advanced Numeracy Tests, Revised Edition* (2008). It achieves this by providing masses more practice material, answers and explanations. Most of the practice material is organized as realistic tests. This means that you can really get down to improving your exam technique and becoming well practised at answering questions under exam-type conditions. Interpretations of your score in these mock tests are offered. These comments are intended only to assist in deciding how much and what sort of practice you should concentrate on. Don't read too much into your score or its interpretation. There is no pass or fail mark in these practice tests and you should not draw conclusions about your suitability for any career or your ability or intelligence generally.

When practising, focus on what you are least good at and keep practising it until you get it right every time. Use the feedback on your score in the mock tests to ensure that you undertake enough of the right kind of practice.

Avoid becoming calculator dependent. Employers want staff who can use a calculator but who can also see when the calculator's answer is incorrect. So revise and sharpen your mental arithmetic, practise estimating the answer by rounding the sums to more convenient figures and using this estimate to confirm the answer given by the calculator.

Use a calculator sparingly when working through this book. In some instances it has been suggested that you do not use a calculator for all or some of the tests. In some real tests a calculator will be provided, but not in others, so when practising use one sparingly if at all and primarily only as a tool with which to further your understanding. Note that if a calculator is provided it may have few features – it may not have a squared function, for example, in which case you will have to calculate powers long hand.

Do not rely on this title as your only source of practice material: a proper programme of revision will require more material than contained here. As well as the companion book, *How to Pass Advanced Numeracy Tests* (2008), *How to Pass Data*

Interpretation Tests (2009) will prove valuable for this increasingly common assessment. If you face a battery of tests at the advanced level, including tests of your verbal and abstract reasoning skills, I would recommend that you use the following books published by Kogan Page:

How to Pass Advanced Verbal Reasoning Tests (2008)
How to Pass Diagrammatic Reasoning Tests (2008) – includes practice for data input-
   type questions
How to Pass Graduate Psychometric Tests, 3rd Edition (2007)
The Graduate Psychometric Tests Workbook, 2nd Edition (2010)

Undertake two sorts of practice. First, practise in a relaxed situation, without time constraints. Focus your practice on questions you find challenging and examine any you get wrong to try to work out why.

Once you feel you can answer all the major types of question, practise on the tests in this book. Practise on these questions against a strict time limit and under circumstances as realistic to a real test as you can manage. The aim is to get used to answering the questions under the pressure of time and to build up speed and accuracy while under pressure.

If you are finding it difficult to identify sufficient material relevant to the test that you face, by all means e-mail me at help@mikebryon.com, describing the test, and I will be glad to inform you of any sources that I know.

Psychometric tests and the value of practice

It is common for job seekers to improve their CV or interview technique but few seek to improve their performance in employers' tests. Not enough test candidates realize that they can significantly improve their score through practice.

Your performance in these demanding tests will only stand out from the crowd of other scores if you revise forgotten rules and build up speed and accuracy through practice. You must attend on the day of the test fully prepared and full of confidence and once it begins you must really go for it and keep going until you are told to put your pencil down.

The best candidates are the ones who see the test as an opportunity to demonstrate just how good they really are. Use this and other Kogan Page books to revise your maths and develop a really sharp exam technique. Other candidates will have adopted this strategy so go fully prepared or risk coming a poor second.

Practice makes a significant difference in your performance in this type of test. The motivated candidates who spend the weeks before the exam revising their maths, practising on similar questions and taking realistic mock tests will score better than they would otherwise have done. For some, practice will mean the difference between pass and fail.

If you have always excelled at something other than maths then now is the time to correct the situation. Anyone can master the operations examined in advanced numeracy tests. Some people need a little more time and practice but that goes for everything. Employers want all-round candidates and there are no prizes for being rejected as a great candidate except for the maths!

Occupational psychologists accept that a lack of familiarity with tests, low self-esteem, nervousness or a lack of confidence will result in a lower score. It is equally true to say that hard work, determination and systematic preparation will lead to an improvement in performance.

Avoid any feelings of resentment over the fact that you have to take a test. Concentrate on the opportunities that will follow if you pass. Have confidence in yourself and really try your best.

Your confidence will grow with practice. Practice will also help because it will mean that you make fewer mistakes and work more quickly against the often very tight time constraints. It will ensure that you are familiar with the test demands and enable you to revise forgotten rules and develop a good exam technique. If passing is important to you then you should be prepared to make a major commitment in terms of the amount of time you set aside for practice.

The best-scoring candidate arrives very well prepared. You should attend on the day of your test fully aware of what the test involves, the type of questions it comprises and how long you have. Before the real test begins, the test administrator or the computer program will allow you to review a number of sample questions and describe the process. If you have arrived properly prepared then all of this information should be entirely familiar. In particular you should have already undertaken lots of practice on each type of question described.

It is important to organize your time during the test as otherwise you risk being told that you have run out of time before you have attempted every question. This is where the practice on mock tests really helps. Keep a track on how long you are spending on each question and make sure you are working at a pace that will allow you to attempt every question in the time left. Expect to do the early questions more quickly as every test starts easy and gets progressively more difficult. You have to be accurate but you must also be fast. So revise your mental arithmetic, and estimate answers and modify sums so that the calculations are more convenient; then look to the suggested answers to pick out the correct value. This is how you apply a really effective exam technique. You can only develop one through practice.

Keep going when you find a succession of difficult questions and avoid being delayed trying to pick up points that you really do not stand much chance of getting. The next section may comprise entirely different material for which you are better prepared.

Crude guessing is unlikely to improve your position. Most tests penalize wrong or unanswered questions. For every question that you cannot answer, look to the suggestions and try to rule some out as definitely wrong. If you then guess from the remaining options you may have significantly increased your chance of guessing correctly. Never try less than your best.

If you fail, ask the organization to provide you with some comments on your performance. Straight after the exam, note down the type of question and the level of difficulty. Use the experience to locate practice material and to inform a new programme of practice. Make sure that you concentrate on the areas in which you did less well.

Failing will not prejudice any future applications that you make to the company. There may be rules that mean you cannot apply again immediately. Some companies, for example, require a six-month gap between applications. However, many candidates pass on a second, third or later attempt and go on to enjoy an unimpeded career within the organization.

A key concepts reference

Make sure you are familiar with all the following operations, formulae and terms. They do not represent every operation covered in this book or in advanced numeracy tests but they represent an important start and will serve as an *aide-mémoire* before you take Test 1, which follows.

You are bound to be tested on these key concepts and others besides, so revise them and then practise them until you get them right quickly and every time. Then you will know they represent easy marks in a real test and you are ready to move on to the content of the later practice tests and further operations examined there.

Recognize patterns

Sequence of odd numbers:
1 3 5 7 9 11

Sequence of even numbers:
2 4 6 8 10 12

Sequence of **prime numbers** (has only two factors, 1 and itself):
2 3 5 7 11 13 17 19

To test a number to see if it is a prime number, find its square root and then divide by the prime numbers up to the value of the square root. If none divide exactly it is a prime number.

A list of **whole number factors** to the value of 18 (prime numbers excluded).
Whole number factors of:
4: 1, 2, 4
6: 1, 2, 3, 6
8: 1, 2, 4, 8
9: 1, 3, 9

10: 1, 2, 5, 10
12: 1, 2, 3, 4, 6, 12
14: 1, 2, 7, 14
15: 1, 3, 5, 15
16: 1, 2, 4, 8, 16
18: 1, 2, 3, 6, 9, 18

The first 12 **square numbers**:
1, 4, 9, 16, 25, 36, 49, 64, 81, 100, 121, 144

Remember, square numbers are whole but any number can be squared.

To find the square of a number multiply it by itself.

Learn the first 10 **cubed numbers**:
1, 8, 27, 64, 125, 216, 343, 512, 729, 1,000

1 and 64 are both squared and cubed numbers.

Powers A square number is a whole number raised to the power of 2. A cubed number is a whole number raised to the power of 3.

Numbers can be raised to any power. The values get big very quickly. Use the x^y or y^x functions on a calculator to calculate powers. Be able to recognize the sequence of low value powers:
$2^2 - 2^7$
4, 8, 16, 32, 64, 128

$3^2 - 3^6$
9, 27, 81, 243, 729

$4^2 - 4^5$
16, 64, 256, 1,024

$5^2 - 5^5$
25, 125, 625, 3,125

To multiply powers with common base numbers simply add the powers:
$6^2 \times 6^5 = 6^7$

To divide powers with common base numbers subtract the powers.

Reciprocals If a number is divided into 1 you identify its reciprocal value. Some reciprocal values are better expressed as fractions because as decimals they are re-occurring. Be familiar with the convenient reciprocal values in the range 1–32:

2 = 0.5
4 = 0.25
5 = 0.2
8 = 0.125
10 = 0.1
16 = 0.0625
20 = 0.05
25 = 0.04
32 = 0.03125

The key terms in data interpretation

Mode is the value that occurs most frequently. The mode of the following data is 2 because it occurs five times:

2, 2, 2, 3, 3, 1, 2, 3, 1, 2, 3

The mode value of the following grouped data is the group 11–20:

Data group	Frequency
1–10	3
11–20	4
21–30	3

The **median** is the middle value when all the responses are arranged numerically. The median of the following values is 4:

10, 2, 8, 6, 4, 3, 1

The median divides the data into 2.

Learn the formula:
Median = $\frac{1}{2}$ (n + 1)th value

The **mean** is the numerical average and is found by adding up all the values and dividing the sum by the number of values.

The mean of the following wages is $\frac{60,000}{4} = 15,000$

Wages
12,000
10,000
23,000
15,000

This example illustrates how an exceptionally high (or low) value (here 23,000) can distort the mean.

To approximate the mean of grouped data the mid-point (mid-interval value) of each group can be used.

Range is the distribution between the lowest and highest value. Range is also distorted by exceptional values.

Quartiles divide the distribution into four equal parts.

To identify the lower quartile use the formula:
$\frac{1}{4}$ (n + 1)th value

To identify the upper quartile use:
$\frac{3}{4}$ (n + 1)th value

The **interquartile range** examines only the middle two quartiles so avoids the distortions of exceptional values (these would lie in the upper or lower quartiles).

Minus the lower quartile value from the upper quartile value to obtain the value of the interquartile range.

A **percentile** divides the distribution into 100 equal parts.

If a relationship exists between two items a **correlation** is said to exist. When plotted, a curve or straight line will emerge and is taken as evidence of a correlation.

Distribution of data is often shown as a **standard deviation**. It takes account of all the values and provides an interpretation of the extent to which the data deviates from the mean.

In the workplace, specialist statistical software is likely to be used to calculate the standard deviation. But go to a psychometric test able to recognize the formula used:

$$s = \frac{\sqrt{\Sigma(x - \bar{x})^2}}{n}$$

Percentages To change a decimal into a percentage multiply it by 100. To express a fraction as a percentage again multiply it by 100. To convert a percentage into a decimal divide by 100.

To work out a percentage of something without a calculator try finding 1 per cent of the item and then multiply to get the answer. Alternatively convert it into a decimal or fraction and again multiply it.

Ratios are used to compare quantities. They are expressed in their lowest whole numbers. For example:
If there are 14 beads on a necklace, 6 of which are blue and 8 of which are red, then the ratio between blue and red beads is 6:8, which simplifies to 3:4.

Simple interest is the amount earned or paid on a sum invested (the principal amount). To calculate it you need to know the principal amount, the annual rate of interest and the length of time the interest is earned.

$$\text{Principal} + \frac{(\text{principal} \times \text{rate} \times \text{period})}{100}$$

Compound interest involves the reinvestment of the earned interest, which in future years also earns interest.

If the amount is only for a few years you can calculate the amount to which the principal grows by the end of the period by treating each year as a simple interest calculation and totalling the amount over the period. Otherwise use the formula:

$$\text{Principal} \times \left(1 + \frac{\text{Rate}}{100}\right)^{\text{period}}$$

The measure of whether or not an event will happen is its **probability**. It is measured on a scale of 0–1, where 1 is a certain event, although the probability of an event occurring is also described as a fraction or percentage. It is calculated by dividing:

$$\frac{\text{The number of positive outcomes}}{\text{The number of possible outcomes}}$$

The probability of throwing a coin and it landing head first is 0.5 on the probability scale or $\frac{1}{2}$, 0.5 or even.

In more complex situations **tree diagrams** can be used to calculate probability and to show all possible outcomes. The tree diagram below illustrates all possible outcomes if a disc is drawn from a bag containing 2 red (R), 1 green (G) and 3 white (W) discs and a second disc is drawn from another bag containing 3 green and 1 red disc. The probability of each outcome can be calculated by multiplying the fractions.

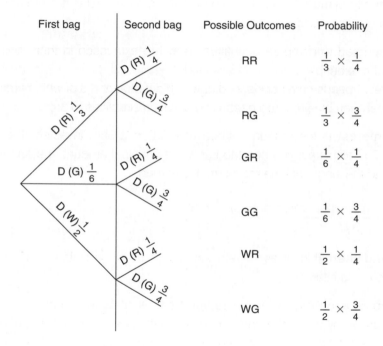

First bag	Second bag	Possible Outcomes	Probability
	D (R) $\frac{1}{4}$	RR	$\frac{1}{3} \times \frac{1}{4}$
D (R) $\frac{1}{3}$	D (G) $\frac{3}{4}$	RG	$\frac{1}{3} \times \frac{3}{4}$
	D (R) $\frac{1}{4}$	GR	$\frac{1}{6} \times \frac{1}{4}$
D (G) $\frac{1}{6}$	D (G) $\frac{3}{4}$	GG	$\frac{1}{6} \times \frac{3}{4}$
	D (R) $\frac{1}{4}$	WR	$\frac{1}{2} \times \frac{1}{4}$
D (W) $\frac{1}{2}$	D (G) $\frac{3}{4}$	WG	$\frac{1}{2} \times \frac{3}{4}$

The elements of geometry

To calculate the area of a **square or rectangle**, multiply the length of its base by its height. The internal angles add up to 360°.

A **triangle** is made up of three straight lines. The internal angles add up to 180°. You calculate its area by:

$\frac{1}{2}$ base × height

The circumference of a **circle** is found by:
C = π × diameter or π × 2 radius

To approximate a circumference multiply the diameter by 3. The answer will be a greater sum.

π can be approximated as 3.14.

The area of a circle is found using:
Area = π × r²

Because it involves the operation of many of the methods just described, questions are sometimes posed requiring you to discover the surface area of a **cylinder**. Imagine a tin of beans! It involves calculating the area of two circles and the wall of the tin, which when opened out is a rectangle. The question may require you to calculate the length of the rectangle from the circumference of the circle. The formulae to use are:

Area of base and lid = 2πr²
Area of rectangle = circumference of lid × height = π × 2r × height
So formula for the surface area of a cylinder = 2πr² + 2πrh

If you know the length of two sides of a right angled triangle then using **Pythagoras' theorem** the length of the third side can be found. Pythagoras' theorem states that the square of the hypotenuse (the sloping side) is equal to the sum of the squares of the two other sides. The theorem can be manipulated to find the length of any side of a right angled triangle.

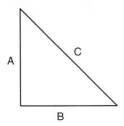

C² = A² + B²
A² = C² − B²
B² = C² − A²

The ratios **sine**, **cosine** and **tangent** are used to find the angles or lengths of sides in right angled triangles. Each links two sides of a right-angled triangle with an angle. You need to relearn the ratios that relate to the particular sides of a triangle to know which ratio to use in a given situation and use the sin, cos and tan functions on a calculator. They are:

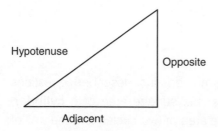

$$\text{Sin } a = \frac{\text{Opposite}}{\text{Hypotenuse}}$$

$$\text{Cos } a = \frac{\text{Adjacent}}{\text{Hypotenuse}}$$

$$\text{Tan } a = \frac{\text{Opposite}}{\text{Adjacent}}$$

The **volume** of a cuboid is found by multiplying its length, width and height. The volume of a square is the cube of one side.

The volume of a sphere is found using the formula:
$V = \frac{4}{3} \pi r^3$

The volume of a cylinder is found using:
$V = \pi r^2 h$

Key quantitative operations

How confident are you in the key numerical skills?

Take this test, benefit from the practice, score yourself and then read the interpretation of how well you did and use it to focus your practice on the areas where you have most to gain.

Advanced numeracy tests take the basic skills for granted. So begin your practice by identifying which if any of these principles you need to relearn. If you feel confident in these operations then use this test to confirm that you already have the necessary key skills and move on to later chapters.

The test reviews the basic operations taken for granted in advanced numeracy tests. The candidates who will pass a psychometric test of their numerical skills will be confident and accurate in all parts of the test and will complete it within the recommended time. They will be able to do this without a calculator.

Later tests provide practice in more complex operations.

Keep revising your mental arithmetic until you are able to complete questions at this level and within this timescale without a calculator.

This is a long test so it is a lot like the real thing in that it is a test of your endurance and stamina as well as your advanced numeracy skills.

Test 1 Key quantitative operations

Test instructions

This test comprises 71 questions.

Allow yourself 45 minutes in which to complete it.

It consists of a series of questions and a number of labelled answers to choose from. Only one of the suggested answers is correct. It is your task to select the suggested answer that you think is correct and record its identifying label in the answer box.

The answer to all questions will be either A, B, C, D or E, depending on the number of suggested answers.

Attempt every question working quickly. If you run out of time, keep working until you have finished all the questions.

Answers and explanations are provided on pages 188–93. An interpretation of your score is offered on pages 230–31.

Remember no calculator is needed.

Do not turn the page until you are ready to begin.

Try to complete the test without interruption.

Q1   Complete the following conversions between fractions, decimals and percentages. Express all fractions in their lowest form.

Fraction	Decimal	Percentage
$^3/_4$		
	0.2	
		60%
	0.375	
$^1/_4$		

Q2   Which of the following fractions is an equivalent to $^1/_4$?

A $^{10}/_{14}$

B $^6/_{42}$

C $^8/_{32}$

D $^3/_{36}$

Answer [   ]

Q3   Which of the following fractions is an equivalent to $^2/_3$?

A $^{37}/_{45}$

B $^{40}/_{55}$

C $^{44}/_{66}$

D $^{15}/_{27}$

Answer [   ]

Q4   What is the value of n in this pair of equivalent fractions:

$^N/_{12}$, $^{18}/_{108}$

A   2

B   3

C   1

D   4

Answer [   ]

Q5 Identify 65 as a fraction of 104 in its simplest form.

A $^3/_5$

B $^5/_8$

C $^7/_9$

D $^1/_2$

Answer

Q6 The sum of $^1/_4$ and $^2/_3$ is:

A 1 and $^1/_{12}$

B $^2/_{12}$

C $^3/_7$

D $^{11}/_{12}$

Answer

Q7 The sum of $^3/_8$ and $^5/_6$ is:

A 1 and $^5/_{24}$

B 1 and $^1/_{14}$

C $^8/_{14}$

D 1 and $^3/_5$

Answer

Q8 The sum of $^1/_2$ and $^1/_6$ is:

A $^2/_{12}$

B $^2/_3$

C $^5/_6$

D $^2/_8$

Answer

Q9   If you subtract $^1/_4$ from $^1/_3$ the answer is:

A $^1/_6$

B $-^1/_{12}$

C $-^1/_6$

D $^1/_{12}$

Answer   ⬚

Q10 $^5/_6$ minus $^3/_{10}$ leaves:

A $^{17}/_{30}$

B $^8/_{15}$

C $^1/_4$

D $^1/_2$

Answer   ⬚

Q11 If you multiply $^2/_5$ by $^5/_6$ you get:

A $^1/_2$

B $^1/_4$

C $^1/_3$

D $^1/_6$

Answer   ⬚

Q12 If you multiply $^2/_7$ by $^3/_4$ you get:

A $^3/_{14}$

B $^1/_4$

C $^5/_7$

D $^3/_7$

Answer   ⬚

Q13 Which number is not a factor of 25?

    A 1

    B 5

    C 12.5

    D 25

Answer

Q14 Which of the following is not a common factor of 12 and 18?

    A 3

    B 2

    C 9

    D 6

Answer

Q15 The sum when 5^2 is multiplied with 5^6 is:

    A 5^{12}

    B 5^4

    C 40

    D 5^8

Answer

Q16 The sum when 6^6 is divided by 6^2 is:

    A -6^3

    B 6^4

    C 6^{12}

    D 6^3

Answer

Q17 What can the formula $\pi \times r \times r$ be used to calculate?

A   The area of a circle

B   The circumference of a circle

C   The diameter of a circle

D   The volume of a sphere

Answer

Q18 What can the formula $\text{Tan } \theta \ \dfrac{\text{Opposite}}{\text{Adjacent}}$ be used to calculate?

A   The length of a cord

B   The surface area of a prism

C   An angle in a right angled triangle

D   An angle in a regular polygon

Answer

Q19 What can the formula $\frac{1}{2} \times b \times h$ be used to calculate?

A   The area of a trapezium

B   The area of a triangle

C   The area of a rectangle

D   The area of a semicircle

Answer

Q20 Which formula would afford the surface area of a cylinder?

A $\frac{3}{4}\pi r^2$

B $\pi r^2 h$

C $\pi \times d \times h$

D $2\pi r^2 + 2\pi rh$

Answer

Q21 Which of the following is not a prime number?

    A 7

    B 11

    C 13

    D 16

Answer

Q22 How many factors does 20 have?

    A 4

    B 5

    C 6

    D 7

Answer

Q23 What is the value of 2^{10}?

    A 20

    B 1,024

    C 512

    D 2,048

Answer

Q24 Which power has the highest value?

    A 2^7

    B 3^5

    C 15^2

    D 6^4

Answer

Q25 Which is the index form of the value $3 \times 3 \times 3 \times 3 \times 3 \times 3$?

    A 3^5

    B 3^6

    C 729

Answer

Q26 Which of the suggestions is not equivalent?

    A 6^2

    B 8^2

    C 2^6

    D 4^3

Answer

Q27 Which number completes the sequence?

    1   4   9   ??   25

    A 18

    B 16

    C 14

    D 10

Answer

Q28 Which of the following is a squared number?

    A 99

    B 130

    C 169

    D 172

Answer

Q29 What is 1.2^2?

 A 2.4

 B 1

 C 1.3

 D 1.44

            Answer [   ]

Q30 A square carpet is $36m^2$. How long are its sides?

 A 5m

 B 7m

 C 4m

 D 6m

            Answer [   ]

Q31 What is 9^3?

 A 1,000

 B 729

 C 512

 D 343

            Answer [   ]

Q32 Which two values are both square and cube numbers?

 A 1

 B 8

 C 27

 D 64

            Answer [   ]

Q33 Which volume is incorrect?

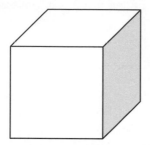

A Cube with sides of 3cm so volume of 27cm³

B Cube with sides of 5cm so volume of 125 cm³

C Cube with sides of 7cm so volume of 216cm³

D Cube with sides of 9cm so volume of 729cm³

Answer _____

Q34 If 75 per cent of a class of 32 children cannot do long division, how many children still need to master this method?

A 7

B 21

C 24

D 14

Answer _____

Q35 If interest was not reinvested, to how much would an investment of £1,000 grow over a 5-year period at a 3 per cent annual rate of interest?

A £150

B £1,150

C £1,159

D £159

Answer _____

Q36 If the interest was compounded annually, to how much to the nearest penny would an investment of £1,000 grow over a 5-year period at a 3 per cent annual rate of interest?

A £1,150.30

B £1,159.27

C £150.30

D £159.27

Answer

Q37 In the right-angled triangle, what is the length of side C?

A 25cm

B 3cm

C 5cm

D 9cm

3 cm

C

4 cm

Answer

Q38 What is the volume of a sphere if it has a radius of 3cm? Treat π as 3.14. Answers are expressed to the nearest whole number.

A 113cm^3

B 268cm^3

C 53cm^3

D 253cm^3

Answer

Q39 The radius of the cylinder is 3cm and its height is 5cm. Treat π as 3.14 and find the volume of the cylinder to the nearest whole cm.

A 47cm^3

B 282cm^3

C 141cm^3

D 28cm^3

Answer

Q40 What is the surface area of a cylinder with a radius of 2cm and a height of 4cm. Again take π as 3.14. All suggested answers have been rounded to the nearest whole cm^2.

   A 50cm^2

   B 18cm^2

   C 25cm^2

   D 75cm^2

Answer [＿＿＿＿]

Q41 In algebraic form the sum of x plus three times y is:

   A $\dfrac{x}{3y}$

   B x(3y)

   C x + 3y

   D Σx = 3Y

Answer [＿＿＿＿]

Q42 In algebraic form four times y squared, divided by 2 times X to the power of 4 is:

   A $\dfrac{4y^2}{2X^4}$

   B $\dfrac{4y \times 4y}{2X \times 4}$

   C $\dfrac{2y^2}{X^4}$

   D $\dfrac{4y \times y}{2X \times X \times X \times X}$

Answer [＿＿＿＿]

Q43 What is the Σxyz if:

$x + 4 = 8$
$4y = 12$
$18 = z + 4$

A 17

B 19

C 21

D 23

Answer

Q44 What is the value of x in $3x - 3 = 18$?

A 7

B 21

C 6

D 9

Answer

Q45 Which equation is the transposition of:

$a = x^2$

A $\frac{a}{\sqrt{x}}$

B $\frac{x}{\sqrt{a}}$

C $\sqrt{x} = a$

D $\sqrt{a} = x$

Answer

Q46 Which linear equation would plot as follows:

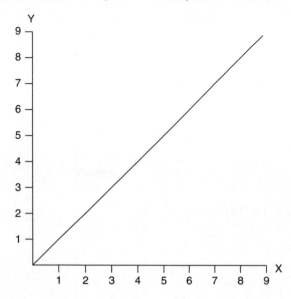

A $y = x^2$

B $y = x$

C $y = 2x$

D $2y = x$

Answer

Q47 Which linear equation would plot as follows:

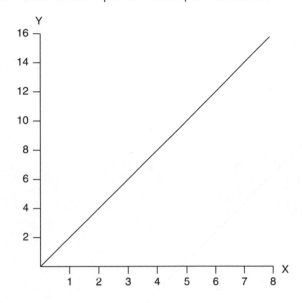

A $y = x^2$

B $y = x$

C $y = 2x$

D $x + y = 6$

Answer

Q48 Which linear equation would plot as follows:

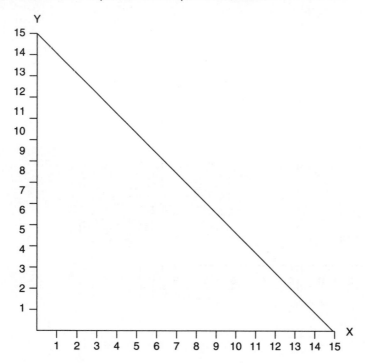

A $x + y = 15$

B $x + 2y = 12$

C $y = x + 1$

D $x + y = 6$

Answer

Q49 Which linear equation would plot as follows:

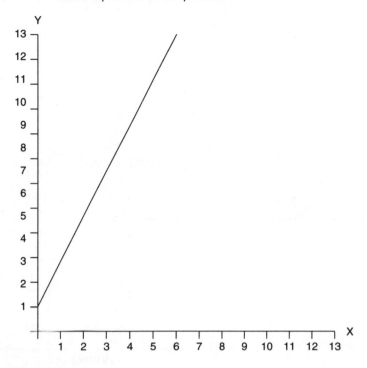

A $x = y - 3$

B $x^2 = y$

C $y = x + 1$

D $y = 2x + 1$

Answer

Q50 What is the equation that is plotted on the graph?

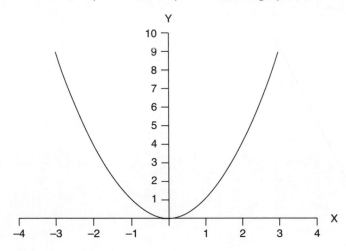

A $x = y^2$

B $x = y^2 + 1$

C $y = x^2$

D $y = x^2 + 1$

Answer

Q51 What is the equation plotted on this graph?

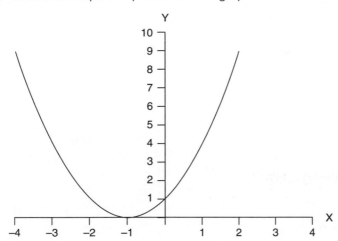

A $x^2 = y + 1$

B $y - 1 = x^2$

C $y = x^2 + 1$

D $y = (x + 1)^2$

Answer

Q52 Which value could x not be if:

$x = <4$

A –5

B 4

C 0

D –3

Answer

Q53 What value could x not have if:

x ≥ 3?

A   −3

B   5

C   3

D   4

Answer _____

Q54 Which of the following is false?

A   −2 < 2

B   2 × 12 > 3 × 6

C   10 × 2 < 8 × 2

D   7 ≥ 7

Answer _____

Q55 Which value is included in the following inequality expression?

2 ≤ x < 3

A   x = 3

B   x = 2

C   x = 4

D   x = 1

Answer _____

Q56 Which value is included in the following inequality expression?

x < −2

A   x = −2

B   x = 0

C   2

D   None of these

Answer _____

Q57 Which value is included in this inequality region?

$-6 < x < -3$

A 0

B -3

C -4

D -6

Answer

Q58 What is the inequality expression that is equal to the shaded region in the graph?

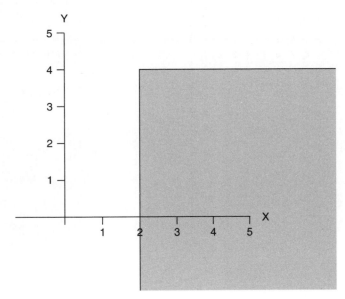

A $\geq 2 \, x \geq 4 \, y$

B $x \geq 2, y \geq 4$

C $x > 2, y \leq 4$

D $x \leq 2, y > 4$

Answer

Q59 Which inequality expression is equal to the shaded region?

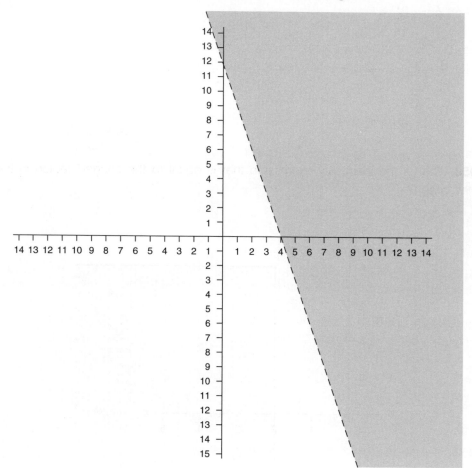

A $y + 3x > 12$

B $y - 3x > 12$

C $y + 3x < 12$

D $y - 3x < 12$

Answer

Q60 Find the mean of the following data:

Responses $\qquad\qquad\Sigma$
13, 13, 13, 14, 15, 16 $\qquad$ 84

A 14

B 13.33

C 13

D 14.33

Answer [ ]

Q61 Find the mean of the following frequency distribution:

Response	Frequency
13	2
14	3
15	6
16	1
	Σ 12

A 14

B 14.5

C 13

D 13.5

Answer [ ]

Q62 Find the modal value for the following data:

Responses $\qquad\qquad\qquad\Sigma$
12, 12, 13, 13, 13, 14, 15, 15 $\qquad$ 107

A 14

B 13.38

C 13

D 12.75

Answer [ ]

Q63 Find the median of the following values:

Responses	Σ
5, 12, 6, 7, 9	39

A   7

B   6

C   9

D   7.8

Answer

Q64 Find the range for the following data:

Results (time: hours minutes)	Σ
1h 12, 1h 09, 1h 03, 1h 20	4h 44

A   0h 20min

B   1h 04.5min

C   0h 17min

D   1h 06min

Answer

Q65 How many respondents indicated less than 4 on the response scale?

Response scale	Cumulative frequency
$0 \leq x < 2$	6
$2 \leq x < 4$	15
$4 \leq x < 6$	28
$6 \leq x < 8$	31
$8 \leq x < 10$	34

A   6

B   9

C   15

D   21

Answer

Q66 In a pack of sweets there are 18 red and 63 green. What is the ratio of red to green sweets?

    A 2:3

    B 1:4

    C 1:7

    D 2:7

Answer

Q67 Which of the following ratios has not been cancelled properly?

    A 105:45 = 7:3

    B 24:56 = 3:7

    C 20:60 = 4:12

    D 36:54 = 2:3

Answer

Q68 An executor is instructed to divide 270 shares between three charities in the ratio 3:2:4. How many shares will each institution receive?

    A 70:40:140

    B 45:30:60

    C 80:60:100

    D 90:60:120

Answer

Q69 What is 30 as a percentage of 120?

    A 40%

    B 20%

    C 33.3%

    D 25%

Answer

Q70 What is 6 per cent of 360?

    A 3.6

    B 21.6

    C 60

    D 2.16

Answer _____

Q71 A supplier increases the charge rate for its services by 4 per cent from a figure of £8 per hour. What is the new charge rate?

    A £8.24

    B £8.32

    C £8.20

    D £8.44

Answer _____

End of test

Accounting and business comprehension

Many employers seek to establish the extent to which candidates are familiar with key business terms. Such a familiarity is one of the principal competencies assumed in many psychometric tests. Tests of data sufficiency, data interpretation, quantitative reasoning and business judgement contain many questions set in a business situation that require the candidate to demonstrate a command of these terms along with the ability to perform the numerical operations being examined.

The chapter provides the opportunity to establish whether or not you have a sufficient comprehension of business terms and to undertake extensive practice in order to enhance your understanding and become familiar with dealing with these terms out of the context of the material in which they normally appear.

The practice questions have been organized into two tests. The first is concerned with fundamental accountancy terms such as depreciation, balance sheet, profit and loss and so on. These terms are in general usage and a competency in them indicates a relatively complex command of the language of business.

The second test examines a very wide range of general business terms. It consists of over 90 questions so in addition to providing an assessment of your comprehension of the language of commerce it also provides realistic practice of a lengthy, challenging test in which you will have to work quickly and maintain your concentration.

Answers and in many instances explanations are provided on pages 193–95. An interpretation of your score is provided on pages 231–32.

Your command of business terms will improve significantly if you practise at this type of question and take time to review your answers and review the questions you get wrong with the benefit of the explanations given.

It will also greatly help if you regularly spend time reading quality business journals and newspapers.

Test 2 Fundamental accounting terms

Test instructions

The following test comprises 33 questions. You are required to indicate which of the suggested answers is most correct.

The test consists of a series of questions and labelled suggested answers to choose from. You are required to select one of the suggested answers as the correct one and to record that answer's identifying label in the answer box.

Attempt all questions in the allowed time and work without interruption or pause.

Example question

A finance company is:

A   A company that has an overdraft facility at a bank or other institution

B   A firm of professional advisors providing advice on financial products

C   A company that loans money to other companies or individuals

D   None of these

Answer | C |

All questions are of the type illustrated in the example above so none require a calculator.

Do not turn the page until you are ready to begin.

Allow yourself 12 minutes to attempt all the questions.

Q1 Accelerated depreciation:

A Is a method that allows greater amounts to be deducted in the early years of the life of an asset

B Assumes equal depreciation during each year of an asset's life

C Is permitted under the straight-line method of depreciation

D None of these

Answer

Q2 Accounts payable are:

A A list of the entities to which a company owes money

B A list of current debtors

C A list of the salaries due

D A list of creditors

Answer

Q3 The accounts receivable ledger is:

A A list of the customers that owe sums to the company, showing each transaction and a balance

B A record of transactions and their effect on the bank account balance

C An accounting record of all payments received

D A type of financing in which the money owed to a company is used as the security for working capital advanced by a bank

Answer

Q4 Apportionment by direct allocation means:

A To allocate taxable income on a basis proportionate to payroll expense

B To allocate income and expenditure item by item

C To allocate expenditure and income by an agreed formula

D None of these

Answer

Q5 Which of the following is not true of a balance sheet?

A The debt and credit side must be equal

B The credit side shows liabilities

C It provides a summary of the revenue, costs and expenses

Answer [   ]

Q6 In accounting, the year end is:

A The date when dividends are announced

B The end of the fiscal year

C The date when an accounting year ends

D New Year's Eve

Answer [   ]

Q7 A trial balance is:

A An empirical method for testing scientific theories

B A list of debits and credits, which should balance

C A record of the balance of payments of a country with the rest of the world

D A small batch of a new product to test a production line

Answer [   ]

Q8 Single entry bookkeeping involves:

A Journals

B Ledgers

C Balancing debits and credits

D None of these

Answer [   ]

Q9 The payee is:

A The organization or person to whom a debt should be paid

B Abbreviation for the 'pay as you earn' excise duty

C The person who pays a bill

Answer [   ]

Q10 Which of the following is still to be deducted from an operating profit?

    A The cost of sales

    B The pay of employees

    C The cost of depreciation and taxes

    D The cost of premises and rents

                      Answer

Q11 Net worth is:

    A The value of someone's assets

    B A person's salary after tax

    C The amount that the value of an asset exceeds liabilities

    D The return on an investment

                      Answer

Q12 A journal is:

    A A tradesperson

    B A book of accounts

    C A record of a transaction

    D A ledger

                      Answer

Q13 Accrued income is:

    A The amount of interest payable on a loan

    B The interest derived from an investment

    C The rate of interest net of taxes

    D Interest on credit cards

                      Answer

Q14 Intercompany transactions are:

A Trading activities between companies that are a part of the same group of companies

B Business to business transactions

C Trading events that do not count as earnings

D None of these

Answer

Q15 A study that would precede the sale of a company and would test the validity of the available financial information is called:

A Audit inspection

B Full disclosure

C Force majeure

D Due diligence

Answer

Q16 The paying out of money to partially clear debts is:

A A cash distribution

B A disbursement

C A discharge

D A deferment

Answer

Q17 The term for someone or an organization to which money is owed is:

A Creditor

B Credit

C Debtor

D Debt

Answer

Q18 To write down an asset is:

A   To enter it on to an accounting system

B   To transfer the balance of an account on to a loss account

C   To record an asset's decrease in value

D   To increase the recorded value of an asset

Answer

Q19 A term that means a receivable that is unlikely to be paid is:

A   Unearned income

B   An unlimited liability

C   Tax deductible

D   An uncollectable account

Answer

Q20 The process of resolving a difference between two accounts is called:

A   Regressive analysis

B   Accounting

C   An adjustment

D   A reconciliation

Answer

Q21 An auditor reports a specific uncertainty by adding to his or her statement:

A   An opinion

B   A reservation

C   A ruling

D   A qualification

Answer

Q22 Net income divided by net sales gives:

    A The revenue

    B Taxable income

    C Tax profit margin

    D The gross turnover

Answer [   ]

Q23 To post a debit or credit is to:

    A Balance it

    B Transfer it from the journal to the ledger

    C Reconcile it

    D Enter it on a journal

Answer [   ]

Q24 Total sales before for example deducting returns and discounts is:

    A Net sales

    B Gross sales revenue

    C Gross sales

    D Sales before costs of sales

Answer [   ]

Q25 Which of the following is not an example of a fixed cost?

    A Taxes

    B Insurance

    C Materials

    D Rent

Answer [   ]

Q26 Another term meaning net worth is:

A   Profit

B   Gross value

C   Equity

D   Net income

Answer

Q27 Which of the following is not an example of earned income?

A   Basic wage before commission

B   Tips

C   Commission

D   Cash dividend

Answer

Q28 A payment by cash is called:

A   A receivable

B   A disbursement

C   A revenue

D   An income

Answer

Q29 In double entry bookkeeping, debits:

A   Increase expenses and decrease revenue

B   Decrease expenses and increase revenues

C   Increase liabilities and decrease assets

D   None of these

Answer

Q30 In double entry bookkeeping, a credit:

A   Increases expenses and decreases revenues

B   Decreases expenses and increases revenues

C   Increases liabilities and increases assets

D   None of these

Answer [   ]

Q31 The difference between sales and cost of sales is:

A   Net profit

B   Taxable profit

C   Profit before tax

D   Gross profit

Answer [   ]

Q32 The cost to acquire goods or services makes it:

A   An asset

B   A revenue

C   A liability

D   None of these

Answer [   ]

Q33 The net amount shown as the worth of an asset is called:

A   Value in use

B   Value added

C   Depreciation

D   Book value

Answer [   ]

End of test

Test 3 Business comprehension

Test instructions

The following test comprises 95 questions. This makes it a test of endurance as well as a test of comprehension.

You are required to indicate which of the suggested answers is most correct.

The test consists of a series of questions and labelled suggested answers to choose from. You are required to select one of the suggested answers as the correct one and to record that answer's identifying label in the answer box. This means that the answer to all the questions will be either A, B, C or D, depending on the number of suggested answers.

Attempt all questions in the allowed time and work without interruption or pause.

A calculator is not required.

Answers and many explanations are provided on pages 195–202 and an evaluation of your score is provided on pages 232–33.

Allow yourself 50 minutes to attempt all the questions.

Do not turn the page until you are ready to begin.

Q1 A liability without limit or fault:

A   Results from negligence

B   Is dependent on an intentional act

C   Is shared jointly with others

D   None of the above

Answer

Q2 Absorbed costs are:

A   Not passed on to the customer

B   Indirect manufacturing costs

C   Always fixed and never variable

D   Costs that have lost their identity

Answer

Q3 The actual cost of something is:

A   The market value

B   The insurance value

C   The amount paid

D   The amount paid plus interest or debt incurred as a result of the purchase

Answer

Q4 An actuary is:

A   Someone qualified in the calculation of exchange rates and currency values

B   Someone qualified in accountancy

C   Someone qualified in the writing of deeds and contracts

D   Someone qualified in the calculation of risk and premiums

Answer

Q5 An example of a conglomerate is:

A   A relationship between two parties

B   The sum total of the whole, ie all outputs during a given period

C   Inefficiency and loss resulting from agglomeration

D   A holding company comprising trading entities active in unrelated areas

Answer [   ]

Q6 Total output in macroeconomics is:

A   All goods and services supplied to the market at a particular price level

B   The goods and services produced by a company during any one financial year

C   The amount of goods or services produced by an individual in his or her lifetime

D   The total amount of spending in an economy at a particular spending level

Answer [   ]

Q7 An example of an amortization term is:

A   A calculation made in life insurance of how long it is expected someone will live

B   The 25 years it takes to pay off the average mortgage through monthly payments

C   A mortgage that requires lower interest and repayment payments in the early years

D   An expression of the amount of risk posed by a business venture

Answer [   ]

Q8   An annuity is:

A   An accounting technique for extending figures for a period of less than one year to a full 12 months

B   A figure giving the value of an insurance policy

C   A term meaning an annual pay increase linked to the rate of inflation

D   An insurance product that pays a fixed amount each year for the life of the insured person or persons

Answer [   ]

Q9   Appropriated expenditure is:

A   An amount set aside to be spent for a particular purpose

B   An expenditure that an auditor identifies as illegal

C   Money spent on property that is owned by someone else

Answer [   ]

Q10 An asset is:

A   Something that will bring an investment return

B   Something that secures a loan

C   Something owned that has a value

D   A member of staff who does a really good job

Answer [   ]

Q11 Money owed that is not collectable is called:

A   Bad debt

B   Insolvent debt

C   Written-off debt

D   Deductible debt

Answer [   ]

Q12 A bond implies:

   A   Twice-yearly income

   B   Tax-free income

   C   The chance to win a million

   D   An obligation to pay

   Answer [   ]

Q13 Yield means the same as:

   A   A return

   B   The return on a business deal

   C   The rate of return

   D   The percentage rate of return

   Answer [   ]

Q14 A zip code is:

   A   A solution to the problem with software recognizing dates past 31 December 1999

   B   A US mail distribution code

   C   A code that regulates the use of property

   D   A way to calculate the Z-scale in statistics

   Answer [   ]

Q15 A hierarchically structured organization is said to be:

   A   A vertical organization

   B   A bureaucracy

   C   Horizontally organized

   D   None of these

   Answer [   ]

Q16 A verbatim report is:

    A Edited to focus on key points

    B Offered with editorial comment

    C A word-for-word account

    D None of these

Answer [ ]

Q17 A troy is:

    A A unit of value in a US system of weights

    B An international standard for quality

    C The unit of value in the gold standard

    D A unit used to measure precious metals

Answer [ ]

Q18 Human resource turnover is calculated by:

    A Ratio to annual sales to net worth

    B Wage costs over a period as a percentage of the total listed

    C Volume of securities traded as a percentage of the total listed

    D Total number of staff divided by the number of new employees during a period

Answer [ ]

Q19 The Standard Industrial Classification is:

    A A numbered system classifying companies by industrial sector

    B A classification of stocks according to the risk associated with industrial activity

    C A system to compare the cost of production in engineering

    D A measure of the performance of the top 100 industrial companies

Answer [ ]

Q20 In economics, which of the following is not an attempt to stabilize markets?

A   Selling the euro to influence its exchange rate

B   Raising interest rates to deter borrowing

C   Training the unemployed in skills wanted by employers

D   Passing on an increase in costs by raising prices

Answer [＿＿＿＿＿]

Q21 To be solvent is to:

A   Have debts that exceed the value of assets

B   Reach an equitable settlement with creditors

C   Be able to pay all debts as they become due

D   Have credit facilities with a bank

Answer [＿＿＿＿＿]

Q22 Ethical investments:

A   Largely consist of a portfolio of shares in for example companies that manufacture armaments and cigarettes

B   Would include the shares of companies that abide with stated social policies

C   Will almost always do less well than unethical investments

D   None of these

Answer [＿＿＿＿＿]

Q23 Shareholder equity is calculated by:

A   Subtracting total liabilities from total assets

B   Subtracting debits from credits

C   Establishing the profit or loss position each year

D   Adding income to the value of assets

Answer [＿＿＿＿＿]

Q24 In business, 'biannual' means:

A   Once a year

B   Every two years

C   Twice a year

Answer

Q25 The term 'seed money' is used by which of the following:

A   Venture capitalists

B   Landlords

C   Actuaries

D   Notaries

Answer

Q26 Security means:

A   An evaluation of a credit or investment risk

B   A non-taxable earning received by a landlord at the beginning of a lease

C   Someone in uniform standing by a supermarket till

D   Something of value offered by a debtor

Answer

Q27 Intellectual royalty:

A   Means ownership of an intellectual product such as a computer program

B   Means that the author asserts him- or herself as the originator of an original idea

C   Is the proceeds from permitting others to use your property

D   Means none of these

Answer

Q28 Underwriting risk is created by:

    A An increase in exchange price

    B A new share issue not selling

    C Inflation

    D Adverse government decisions

Answer [   ]

Q29 An example of revenue is:

    A A company's gross sales

    B An individual's tax liabilities

    C A company's corporation tax bill

    D A business's net sales

Answer [   ]

Q30 A restrictive covenant is:

    A A legal device to limit free trade

    B An agreement to preserve the status quo until a court can give a matter full consideration

    C An order by a court

    D A limitation to the property rights of an owner written into the deeds

Answer [   ]

Q31 To rescind on a contract without risk of penalty could occur in which of the following situations?

    A When you provide written notice that you intend to rescind on the agreement

    B When a court nullifies the contract

    C If the contract were verbal and not written

    D None of these

Answer [   ]

Q32 The widely accepted definition of the point at which an economy is in recession is:

A When economic activity as measured by gross domestic product starts to decline

B When unemployment rises above 3 per cent of the economically active population

C When gross domestic production declines for two consecutive quarters

D When retail prices fall for a period in excess of 12 consecutive months

Answer [   ]

Q33 A rally means:

A Prices increase rapidly

B Profits are up markedly

C Confidence increases noticeably

D Speculative investors have rushed to the market

Answer [   ]

Q34 Quality assurance is:

A A management method that seeks to ensure the production of high-quality services or products

B An international classification of quality

C A process of control that seeks consistent high quality in manufacturing

D Small groups of employees meeting to seek improvements in production methods

Answer [   ]

Q35 Proxy means:

A A display of foresight

B A person authorized to vote or act for another

C How you are viewed by others

D A lease assigned to another

Answer [   ]

Q36 Pro rata means:

A   Something for something

B   For the duration of one's life

C   A qualified opinion

D   Proportionate allocation

Answer [   ]

Q37 The generally assumed relation between risk and return is a:

A   Direct correlation

B   Negative correlation

C   Positive correlation

D   Zero correlation

Answer [   ]

Q38 A poison pill is:

A   A legal document that details the case for the plaintiff's allegations

B   A slang term for a letter of redundancy

C   A device that makes a company's shares less attractive to an unwanted acquirer

D   The term used by the Securities and Exchange Commission when they name an insider trader

Answer [   ]

Q39 Petrodollars are:

A   Dollars spent on development projects in the oil-producing countries

B   Money earned from the sale of oil

C   The name for rich Texans who made their money in oil

D   Dollars paid to oil-producing countries and deposited in Western banks

Answer [   ]

Q40 'Permutations' means:

    A Different subgroups that can be formed from a single sample

    B Perks of the job such as company cars and health club memberships

    C Changes in attitude

    D Alternative plans adopted when plan A fails

Answer

Q41 The statement 'patent pending':

    A Gives the right to exclude others from making or selling a product

    B Indicates that the Patent Office is deciding if the product is patentable

    C Indicates that the owner has a legal monopoly for a fixed period of time

    D Means that the Patent Office is about to issue a patent

Answer

Q42 A participation loan is:

    A High-interest, high-risk borrowing

    B A loan that pays a dividend to the borrower if payments are made on time

    C One where both the lender and the borrower share the risks and profits equally

    D A loan made by more than one lender

Answer

Q43 Parkinson's law states that:

    A Whatever can go wrong will

    B Improved working conditions lead to increases in productivity and quality

    C All organizations will become moribund

    D Employee consultation aids competitiveness and invention

Answer

Q44 A paradigm shift is:

A Panic buying or selling that leads to a major change in price

B A seismic change in business or buying practices that were previously universally accepted

C The move from a market in which pure competition exists to one of a monopoly

D When a corporation is split into two or more smaller business units

Answer [   ]

Q45 An oligopoly is:

A A market dominated by a few major sellers

B A state of pure competition

C A market in which a cartel operates

D A market controlled by one seller

Answer [   ]

Q46 A notary public is:

A A not-for-profit organization that undertakes good works

B An officer authorized to administer oaths

C The publicized plans for the development of a building plot

D An official appointed to act as a representative of the general public when they have a complaint

Answer [   ]

Q47 Niche marketing is:

A Marketing directly to the prospective customer

B Marketing to a particular portion of the whole market

C The promotion of goods at the point of sale

D Marketing directed at the most lucrative sections of the market

Answer [   ]

Q48 Negative amortization occurs when:

    A The repayments on a loan fail to cover the interest charged

    B A borrower pays a loan off early

    C Repayments exceed interest charged, so reducing the capital sum owed

    D None of these

Answer

Q49 An example of a moratorium is:

    A A factor used to estimate a value

    B An agreed delay in the repayment of a debt

    C A chart showing the rate of death by age of a given population

    D A period when the gross domestic product shows no growth

Answer

Q50 Leverage means:

    A Borrowing money to increase the amount available for an acquisition

    B The dock charge for unloading ships

    C Forcing a company or individual to change its practices

    D Adding to an executive team to make it more effective

Answer

Q51 Incorporation in the USA is the same as:

    A Limited warranty in the USA

    B Limited liability in the EU

    C A limited company in the UK

    D A limited partnership in Italy

Answer

Q52 Legal tender is:

   A   An opinion given by a professional

   B   A bid to win a government contract

   C   A competitive tendering process that conforms to national laws

   D   Legally acceptable kinds of money

   Answer [   ]

Q53 A legal entity is:

   A   A person under the legal age of consent

   B   A licence to offer a particular service

   C   An interest protected by law

   D   An organization that can enter into a contract

   Answer [   ]

Q54 Last in first out is:

   A   A law of supply and demand

   B   The time lag between an order and its delivery

   C   A way to identify people for redundancy

   D   The way that computer memory is executed

   Answer [   ]

Q55 Another way to describe the setting of an important precedent is:

   A   Legislation

   B   A board members' resolution at an extraordinary shareholders' meeting

   C   A landmark decision

   D   Queen's Counsel opinion

   Answer [   ]

Q56 Kudos means:

A Satisfaction

B Recognition

C A good monetary return

D None of these

Answer

Q57 An obligation that can be enforced against all parties equally or anyone separately is called:

A A joint specification

B Joint and several

C A joint liability

D None of these

Answer

Q58 A graph illustrating an expected turnaround in a market is called:

A A U-turn

B A Kondratieff wave

C An upturn

D A J curve

Answer

Q59 'In perpetuity' means:

A A physical thing

B An interest-only loan

C For ever

D For a lifetime

Answer

Q60 Pull inflation is likely to happen when:

A   Too much money chases too few goods

B   Spending increases

C   The cost of raw materials rises

D   The market is flooded by too many goods

Answer _____

Q61 Demand for luxury goods is:

A   Highly inelastic

B   As elastic as crude oil

C   Highly elastic

D   As elastic as any other purchase

Answer _____

Q62 'Economic life' can be defined as:

A   Gross individual product

B   The period over which the original cost has been fully written off

C   When a resource's economic value falls below 50 per cent of its replacement cost

D   The period during which income generated exceeds the operating costs

Answer _____

Q63 The effect where an increase in the level of production creates a reduction in unit cost is called:

A   Economic efficiency

B   Economy of scale

C   Production rate curve

D   Scale relationship

Answer _____

Q64 An auction in which prices start high and then bid downwards is called:

   A   Double-sided auction

   B   Reserve price auction

   C   Dutch auction

   D   County auction

   Answer [   ]

Q65 Credo is:

   A   A business philosophy

   B   A critical path

   C   A type of high-yield bond

   D   The most commonly occurring value in a data set

   Answer [   ]

Q66 The term to describe a non-profit-producing part of an organization is:

   A   Department

   B   Echelon

   C   Cost centre

   D   Head office

   Answer [   ]

Q67 Cereals and metals are termed:

   A   Raw materials

   B   Commodities

   C   Aggregates

   D   Essentials

   Answer [   ]

Q68 The acceptance of risk in return for payment is:

   A   Underwriting

   B   Transaction risk management

   C   Risk analysis

   D   Risk premium

Answer

Q69 An evaluation of the internal controls of a business is called:

   A   An audit trail

   B   A test of reasonableness

   C   A procedural audit

   D   Systems analysis

Answer

Q70 A low-priced speculative share is called:

   A   Junior shares

   B   Futures

   C   Penny shares

   D   Junk stock

Answer

Q71 Paper profit is:

   A   The before-tax gain from selling shares

   B   The amount owned but not yet collected

   C   The current value minus the purchase price

   D   The ability to produce net income

Answer

Q72 A big factor in stock inventory risk is:

    A Input price fluctuations

    B Obsolescence

    C Wear and tear

    D Floods and fire

Answer

Q73 A managed portfolio of investments that issues its own shares to investors is called:

    A A municipal bond

    B A trust fund

    C A preferred stock fund

    D A mutual fund

Answer

Q74 A calculation to show the change in total cost as a result of an increase in output is called:

    A Marginal cost analysis

    B Cost inventory

    C A moving average calculation

    D Profit modelling

Answer

Q75 In international trade a device used to guarantee that the seller of goods is paid when the goods are delivered is called:

    A An intercompany account

    B A bill of sale

    C A letter of credit

    D A purchase order

Answer

Q76 ISO9000 is:

A   A quality standard for international manufacturers

B   A computer operating system

C   The acronym for the Institute of Standards and Operations

D   The Japanese standard for continuous improvement

Answer

Q77 Pension funds, insurance companies and so on that trade large volumes of shares are called:

A   Venture capitalists

B   Institutional investors

C   Big hitters

D   Market makers

Answer

Q78 A company is registered to operate under UK and US laws if it:

A   Has limited liability

B   Has an exclusive name

C   Has paid in capital

D   Is incorporated

Answer

Q79 To protect against losses from downward price movements is to:

A   Hedge

B   Pool

C   Pay off

D   None of these

Answer

Q80 The value of a company's name and reputation is called its:

A   Investiture

B   Going concern

C   Shareholders' fund

D   Goodwill

Answer

Q81 When a company permits others to use its name and to sell its products it has granted a:

A   Franchise

B   Licensee

C   Joint venture

D   Takeover

Answer

Q82 An example of an excise tax is:

A   Corporation tax

B   Tax on fuel

C   Inheritance tax

D   Income tax

Answer

Q83 When a company sells its accounts receivable to a bank it is called:

A   Factoring

B   Cashflowing

C   Turnover loan

D   Credit line

Answer

Q84 Stealing from the petty cash box is:

A   A non-business expense deduction

B   Embezzlement

C   Obsolescence

D   An extraordinary item

Answer

Q85 A business owned by its employees and/or customers is a:

A   Trust

B   Not-for-profit organization

C   Cooperative

D   Closed corporation

Answer

Q86 A product distinguished from others in a market by its name or label is:

A   An image

B   A market leader

C   A brand

D   A logo

Answer

Q87 A critical path is:

A   A record of all the types of comment received by a customer service department

B   The sequential actions required to reach a decision

C   The key stages in a complaints process

D   The most effective route through a decision tree

Answer

Q88 Goods sold in plain packaging without promotional logo are called:

A   Supermarket own brands

B   Value lines

C   Generic products

D   Essential products

Answer [   ]

Q89 Golden parachutes are:

A   Inducements to discourage staff from leaving

B   Money paid to attract staff to a company

C   Sums paid when a company realizes a higher share price

D   Payments made when staff leave through no fault of their own

Answer [   ]

Q90 When continuing to apply resources to an unprofitable or low-profit venture you incur:

A   A high opportunity cost

B   Poor positioning

C   Low self-esteem

D   Shareholder objections

Answer [   ]

Q91 A patented medicine is an example of:

A   An undifferentiated product

B   A niche product

C   A proprietary product

D   A trade mark

Answer [   ]

Q92 Which of the following is an example of a brown good?

    A A television

    B A washing machine

    C A sofa

    D A mobile phone

Answer [   ]

Q93 Bundling is a strategy in:

    A Accountancy

    B Information technology

    C Selling

    D Procurement

Answer [   ]

Q94 When a company buys up its supplier, this is an example of:

    A Critical path management

    B Competitiveness

    C Hostile takeover

    D Vertical integration

Answer [   ]

Q95 The push strategy in marketing places greatest weight on:

    A Advertising

    B Trade representatives

    C Branding

    D Discount coupons

Answer [   ]

End of test

Geometry and further quantitative operations

These tests comprise 50 questions each. Answers and explanations are found on pages 202–211. An interpretation of your score in each test is provided on pages 233–36.

You will almost certainly have to revise your numeracy skills with some of these questions! Having said this, the questions are structured so as to lead you through the stages of complexity and are all relevant to the demands of psychometric tests of numeracy.

These tests provide a realistic experience of the challenge real advanced numeracy tests represent especially in terms of the sheer hard work and concentration that is required. To do well, you will have to try hard and work quickly.

Some of the questions require the use of a scientific calculator. If, in the exam you face, a calculator is not allowed, then all the raw data will be provided in the question. However, the methodology will remain the same. Practise until you are able to recognize when it is faster to calculate in your head than on a calculator and take care not to become calculator dependent.

The first test comprises 50 questions of geometry. It should be particularly useful for candidates of GMAT, the test used by business schools to select students for MBA courses, and affords practice in the geometric operations from the fundamental (and straightforward) characteristics of squares to calculations of, for example, the length and angle of planes and arcs.

The second test comprises another 50 questions relevant to general quantitative tests and tests of data interpretation and business judgement. It builds on some of the concepts covered in the diagnostic Test 1, for example prime numbers, factors, percentages and ratios. It then moves through subjects like probability, and on to advanced concepts such as the calculation of standard deviation.

Test 4 A test of geometry

Test instructions

This test consists of 50 questions.

You are allowed 40 minutes in which to complete it.

The test consists of a series of questions and labelled suggested answers to choose from. You are required to select one of the suggested answers as the correct one and to record that answer's identifying label in the answer box.

Example question

The volume of a cube with sides of 3cm is:

A 64cm^3

B 8cm^3

C 27cm^3

D 125cm^3

Answer | C |

Attempt the first 30 questions without a calculator.

Attempt all questions in the allowed time and work without interruption or pause.

Do not turn the page until you are ready to begin the test.

Q1   If 4 squares each 4cm^2 are formed into a rectangle what would be the length of the new shape's longest side?

A   8cm

B   4cm

C   2cm

D   6cm

Answer

Q2   AB = BD = DA. What is angle a?

A   180°

B   60°

C   30°

D   120°

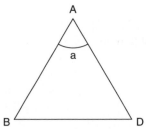

Answer

Q3   What is the length of each side of the cube if it has a cubic area of 64cm^3?

A   2cm

B   6cm

C   8cm

D   4cm

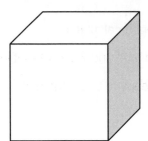

Answer

Q4 Find the size of angle x.

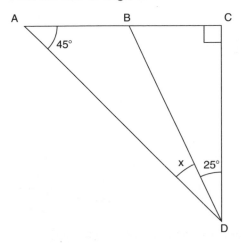

A   30°

B   25°

C   20°

D   15°

Answer

Q5 In the illustrated isosceles triangle, what are the values of angles x and y?

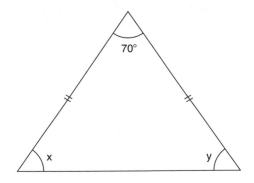

A   60°, 50°

B   70°, 40°

C   90°, 20°

D   55°, 55°

Answer

Q6   Find the missing angles in the kite.

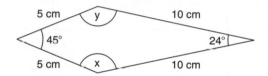

A   145.5°

B   67.5°

C   78°

D   156°

Answer

Q7   What is the size of angle y if the two intersecting lines are straight?

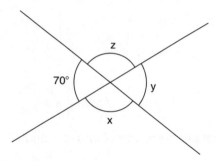

A   35°

B   55°

C   70°

D   110°

Answer

Q8 If you were to try and construct triangles of the following dimensions, which is impossible in that it cannot be drawn or constructed?

A	△ABC where	AB = 3cm	BC = 4cm	CA = 3cm
B	△ABC where	AB = 6cm	BC = 2cm	CA = 9cm
C	△ABC where	AB = 11cm	BC = 8cm	CA = 14cm
D	△ABC where	AB = 5cm	BC = 5cm	CA = 5cm

Answer [   ]

Q9 If lines A and B are parallel, what is the value of angle x?

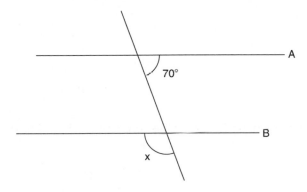

A   110°

B   90°

C   20°

D   60°

Answer [   ]

Q10 Which angle will be the smallest?

A

B

C

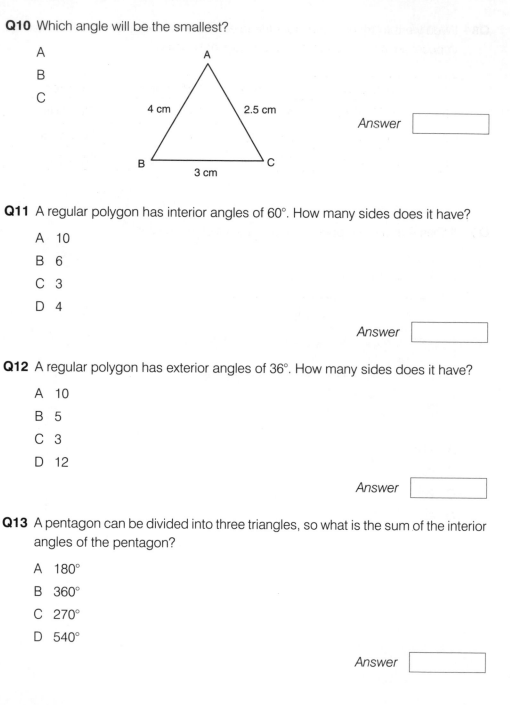

4 cm   2.5 cm

B   3 cm   C

Answer

Q11 A regular polygon has interior angles of 60°. How many sides does it have?

A   10

B   6

C   3

D   4

Answer

Q12 A regular polygon has exterior angles of 36°. How many sides does it have?

A   10

B   5

C   3

D   12

Answer

Q13 A pentagon can be divided into three triangles, so what is the sum of the interior angles of the pentagon?

A   180°

B   360°

C   270°

D   540°

Answer

Q14 What are the exterior angles of a hexagon?

 A 90°

 B 36°

 C 60°

 D 45°

Answer

Q15 Which of the following is not an example of a quadrilateral?

 A Trapezium

 B Rhombus

 C Square

 D They are all quadrilaterals

Answer

Q16 If a pentagon can be divided into three triangles, how many triangles can an octagon be divided into?

 A 5

 B 6

 C 7

 D 8

Answer

Q17 What is the circumference of a circle with a radius of 5cm (take π as 3.14)?

 A 62.8cm

 B 3.14cm

 C 15.7cm

 D 31.4cm

Answer

Q18 What is the circumference of a circle with a diameter of 6cm (take π as 3.14)?

    A   37.68cm

    B   18.84cm

    C   113.04cm

    D   None of these

Answer [＿＿＿＿＿]

Q19 What is the radius of a circle with a circumference of 31.4cm (take π as 3.14)?

    A   10cm

    B   3.14cm

    C   7.5cm

    D   5cm

Answer [＿＿＿＿＿]

Q20 What is the area of a circle with a radius of 3cm (take π as 3.14)?

    A   29.57cm^2

    B   6cm^2

    C   28.26cm^2

    D   None of these

Answer [＿＿＿＿＿]

Q21 What is the area of a circle with a diameter of 10cm (take π as 3.14)?

    A   78.5cm^2

    B   314cm^2

    C   31.4cm^2

    D   None of these

Answer [＿＿＿＿＿]

Q22 What is the area of a circle with a circumference of 25.12cm (take π as 3.14)?

A   200.96cm^2

B   75.36cm^2

C   50.24cm^2

D   None of these

Answer

Q23 What is the area of a circle with a circumference of 21cm (take π as 3)?

A   147cm^2

B   36.75cm^2

C   198cm^2

D   None of these

Answer

Q24 What is the volume of a sphere with a radius of 3cm (treat π as 3.14)?

A   282.6cm^3

B   28.26cm^3

C   11.304cm^3

D   113.04cm^3

Answer

Q25 What is the volume of a hemisphere with a radius of 3cm (treat π as 3.14)?

A   14.13cm^3

B   28.26cm^3

C   56.52cm^3

D   113.04cm^3

Answer

Q26 What is the surface area of the cuboid?

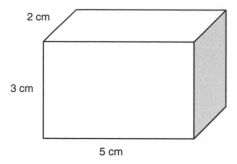

2 cm

3 cm

5 cm

A   30cm^2

B   45cm^2

C   62cm^2

D   70cm^2

Answer

Q27 What is the volume of the cuboid illustrated in Q26?

A   30cm^3

B   45cm^3

C   62cm^3

D   70cm^3

Answer

Q28 A pipe has a radius of 12m and is 60m long. What is its volume (take π as 3.14)?

A   Less than 25,000m^3

B   Less than 250m^3

C   Over 250,000m^3

D   More than 25,000m^3

Answer

Q29 What is the area of the shaded sector on the pie chart? Take the radius to be 3cm and π to be 3.14.

A 31.4cm^2

B 2.826cm^2

C 28.26cm^2

D None of these

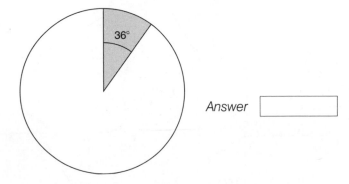

Answer [   ]

Q30 If the radius of the circle is 5cm, how long is the arc marked on its circumference? As usual, treat π as 3.14.

A 7.35cm

B 3.41cm

C 68.2cm

D 6.28cm

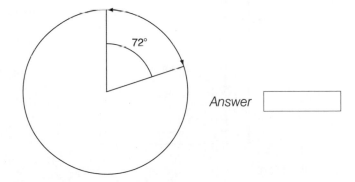

Answer [   ]

Q31 What is the surface area of a cylinder with a radius of 5cm and a height of 6cm (treat π as 3.14)?

A 219.8cm^2

B 204.1cm^2

C 345.4cm^2

D None of these

Answer [   ]

Q32 What is the area of square x?

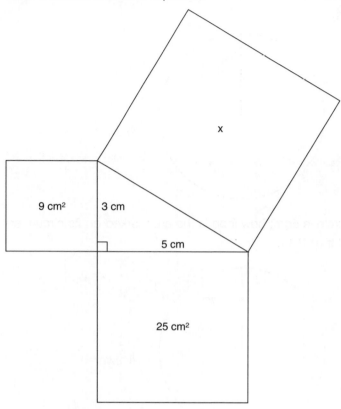

A   34cm²

B   5.8cm²

C   16cm²

D   8cm²

Answer [   ]

Q33 Calculate the length of the hypotenuse of a right-angled triangle where the sum of the square of the other two sides equals 25cm²:

A   6cm

B   5cm

C   4cm

D   3cm

Answer [   ]

Q34 Calculate the length of x in the illustrated right-angled triangle:

A 5cm

B 4cm

C 7cm

D 6cm

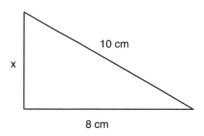

Answer

Q35 Calculate the length of the line drawn on a centimetre-squared grid.

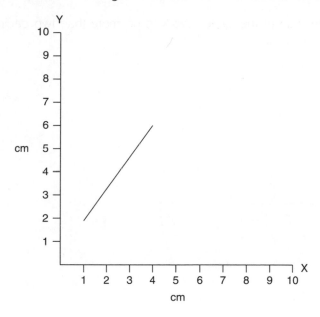

A 4cm

B 7cm

C 8cm

D 5cm

Answer

Q36 Calculate the distance between the following points on the same centimetre-squared grid:

(3,2) (8,14)

A   12cm

B   5cm

C   13cm

D   9cm

Answer

Q37 What is the circumference of the circle? Work to no more than two decimal places.

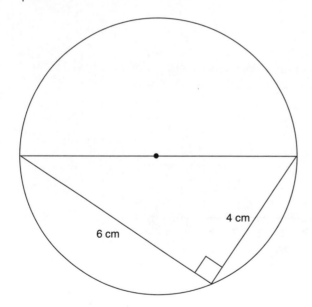

A   18.63cm

B   22.63cm

C   20.63cm

D   None of these

Answer

Q38 Is the following a right-angled triangle?

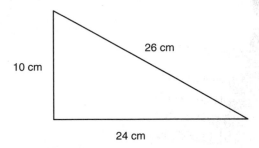

A   Yes

B   No

C   Cannot tell

Answer

Q39 If angle a is given, which ratio would you use to find the length of x?

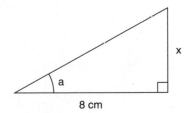

A   Sine

B   Cosine

C   Tangent

Answer

Q40 If angle a is given, which ratio would you use to find the length of x?

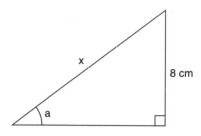

A   Sine

B   Cosine

C   Tangent

Answer

Q41 Which of the following would give you the size of angle a?

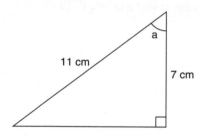

A   Sin a^{-1} 7/11

B   Cos a^{-1} 7/11

C   Tan a^{-1} 7/11

Answer

Q42 Find the length of x:

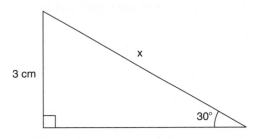

A   5cm

B   3cm

C   6cm

D   10cm

Answer

Q43 Find the length of y:

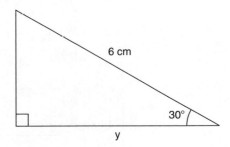

A   5.19cm

B   5cm

C   4.22cm

D   3cm

Answer

Q44 What is the circumference of semicircle x? Work to no more than three decimal places and take π as 3.14. Express your answer to the nearest whole cm.

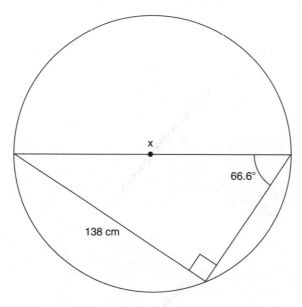

A   236cm

B   138cm

C   150cm

D   387cm

Answer

Q45 Calculate the circumference of the circle. Work to two decimal places. Take π as 3.14.

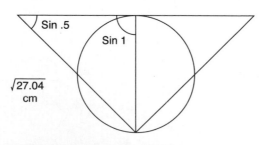

A   8.164cm   B   28.07cm

C   18.98cm   D   4.47cm

Answer

Q46 What is the angle between the planes A,B,C,D and A,F,G,D?

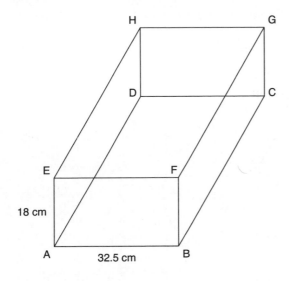

A   29°   B   52°
C   61°   D   45°

Answer [   ]

Q47 For the box illustrated in Q46 find the length of the diagonal AG. Take the length of side BC to be 25cm.

A   32.05cm

B   37.15cm

C   35.41cm

D   44.78cm

Answer [   ]

Q48 Island A is 3 miles due east of island B and 4 miles due south of island C. What is the distance between islands B and C?

A   5 miles

B   12 miles

C   3 miles

D   4 miles

Answer [   ]

Q49 Calculate the size of a, using the cosine rule (not the same as ratio).

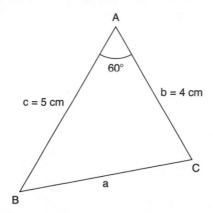

A 3.80cm

B 4.58cm

C 19.49cm

Answer

Q50 What is the length of the perimeter of the triangle?

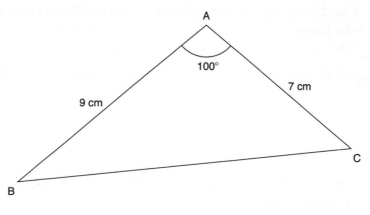

A 26.40cm   B 11.52cm

C 28.32cm   D 12.32cm

Answer

End of test

Test 5 A further test of quantitative operations

Test instructions

This test consists of 50 questions.

You are allowed 40 minutes in which to complete it.

The test consists of a series of questions and labelled suggested answers to choose from. You are required to select one of the suggested answers as the correct one and to record that answer's identifying label in the answer box.

Example question

Convert 44% into a fraction and express it in its lowest form:

A $^{44}/_{100}$

B $^{22}/_{50}$

C $^{11}/_{25}$

D None of these

Answer | C |

Only use a calculator when absolutely necessary! Instead practise rounding figures to more convenient sums and estimating.

Attempt all questions in the allowed time and work without interruption or pause.

Do not turn the page until you are ready to begin the test.

Q1   Convert $^3/_8$ into a percentage:

   A   57.1%

   B   16.6%

   C   37.5%

   D   33.3%

                                         Answer [   ]

Q2   Convert the ratio 1:3:5 into a percentage. Work to only one decimal place.

   A   11%:33.3%:55.5%

   B   22%:66.6%:111%

   C   10%:30%:60%

                                         Answer [   ]

Q3   Convert $^5/_{16}$ into a percentage (work to one decimal place):

   A   29.3%

   B   31.2%

   C   33.3%

   D   30.3%

                                         Answer [   ]

Q4   Convert $^4/_7$ into a percentage (work to one decimal point):

   A   60.0%

   B   55.3%

   C   51.9%

   D   57.1%

                                         Answer [   ]

Q5   Is 23 a prime number?

   A   Yes

   B   No

                                         Answer [   ]

Q6   What is the highest factor that 12 and 18 both have in common?

A 9

B 3

C 6

D 2

Answer

Q7   What is the only even prime number?

A 10

B 14

C 2

D 4

Answer

Q8   What is the highest factor that both 16 and 22 have in common?

A 2

B 3

C 16

D 8

Answer

Q9   Is 19 a prime number?

A Yes

B No

Answer

Q10 If the price of an item is increased from €150 to €200 what is the nearest whole percentage point increase?

A 33%

B 17%

C 11%

D 25%

Answer

Q11 What is the equity interest of the owner of 100 shares of a company's stock if that company has 10,000 shares outstanding?

A 0.001%

B 0.1%

C 1%

D 10%

Answer

Q12 An illustrated book comprises 938 pages. If the ratio of pages with illustrations to pages without is 6:1, how many illustrated pages does the book contain?

A 536

B 804

C 670

D None of these

Answer

Q13 What is the highest factor that both 48 and 72 have in common?

A 6

B 12

C 18

D 24

Answer

Q14 Is 222 a prime number?

   A Yes

   B No

                                        Answer [＿＿＿＿＿＿]

Q15 Convert the ratio 5:5:6 into a percentage:

   A 20%:20%:60%

   B 31.25%:31.25%:37.5%

   C 25%:25%:50%

   D None of these

                                          Answer [＿＿＿＿＿＿]

Q16 20 is a 1/3 of 1% of what number?

   A 6

   B 60

   C 6,000

   D 600

                                          Answer [＿＿＿＿＿＿]

Q17 The depreciation on a piece of office equipment is written down over three sequential years at the percentages 20%, 30% and 40%. If the original cost was £10,000 what was the book value after the depreciation?

   A £1,000

   B £3,360

   C £3,600

   D £2,240

                                          Answer [＿＿＿＿＿＿]

Q18 A firm's monthly wage bill increased by 3.6% after the annual wage review to a new total of £16,000. What was the original monthly figure? (Suggested answers are expressed to the nearest £.)

A   £15,136

B   £15,424

C   £14,993

D   £15,444

Answer

Q19 Is 337 a prime number?

A   Yes

B   No

Answer

Q20 An inventory reveals that the stock of components has decreased by 16% from an original number of 3,250. What number of components are now recorded in the inventory?

A   2,353

B   2,730

C   520

D   None of these

Answer

Q21 What is the highest factor common to both 135 and 270?

A   2

B   135

C   14

D   9

Answer

Q22 An employment agency reduced the charge for its services by 10% and as a result finds that sales have increased by 30%. By what percentage does turnover increase?

A 19%

B 116%

C 17%

D You cannot tell

Answer

Q23 Find the modal value from the following data:

20, 26, 24, 20, 21, 25

A 20

B 22

C 22.6

D 25

Answer

Q24 Find the median of the following values:

10, 2, 9, 3, 8, 1, 7

A 5

B 7

C 6

D 8

Answer

Q25 Find the lower quartile for the following data:

19, 20, 27, 30, 40, 45, 70, 88, 89, 90, 91

A 19

B 24.75

C 27

D 30

Answer

Q26 Find the interquartile range for the data given in Q25.

A   36

B   62

C   55.5

D   45.5

Answer

Q27 What is the average of the 137 consecutive numbers from 282 through to 419?

A   340.5

B   375

C   325

D   350.5

Answer

Q28 Is 48 a prime number?

A   Yes

B   No

Answer

Q29 A supplier increases prices for two consecutive years by 3%. What is the combined percentage increase?

A   7.1%

B   6.09%

C   6%

D   6.03%

Answer

Q30 What is the sum of all the numbers from 16 through to 60?

    A 1,672

    B 1,748

    C 1,980

    D 1,710

Answer

Q31 Which of the following is true of a multiple of 6?

    A Last digit is even

    B Sum of digits is a multiple of 9

    C Sum of digits is a multiple of 3

    D Last digit is odd

Answer

Q32 The average price of a holiday in Europe is €700 per person while the average price for a holiday in the United States is €900. If three times as many holidays to Europe are sold as holidays to the United States, what is the average price of a holiday overall?

    A €750

    B €800

    C €775

    D €825

Answer

Q33 What is the average of every number from 13 to 80?

    A 40

    B 50

    C 46.5

    D 55

Answer

Q34 Which of the following is true of a multiple of 3?

    A Last digit is always 0

    B Sum of digits is multiple of 3

    C Sum of digits is multiple of 9

    D Last digit is 5 or 0

Answer ☐

Q35 What is the range of possible answers to the sum of two two-digit numbers in the addition below:

$$\begin{array}{r} AB \\ +CD \\ \hline EFG \end{array}$$

    A $99 \leq x \geq 100$

    B $100 \leq x \geq 198$

    C $100 \leq x \geq 999$

    D Impossible to tell

Answer ☐

Q36 How many possible outcomes are there when a six-sided dice is rolled, a coin is tossed and a counter is drawn from a box of 70 red counters?

    A 9

    B 82

    C 78

    D None of these

Answer ☐

Q37 On how many days could it rain in a leap year if the probability of it raining tomorrow is $1/3$?

    A 122 days

    B 366 days

    C 244 days

    D None of these

Answer ☐

Q38 How many three-digit numbers can you form with the numbers 6, 7, 8?

A 9

B 12

C 27

D 6

Answer [   ]

Q39 If the probability of it raining tomorrow is $\frac{1}{4}$, what is the probability of it not raining tomorrow?

A $\frac{3}{4}$

B $\frac{1}{4}$

C $\frac{1}{2}$

D None of these

Answer [   ]

Q40 P and Q are mutually exclusive events. The probability of P occurring is $\frac{2}{5}$ and the probability of Q occurring is $\frac{1}{2}$. What is the probability of both P and Q occurring at the same time?

A $\frac{1}{5}$

B $\frac{9}{10}$

C 1

D None of these

Answer [   ]

Q41 P and Q are mutually exclusive events, where the probability of P occurring is $\frac{2}{5}$ and the probability of Q occurring is $\frac{1}{2}$. What is the probability of either P or Q occurring?

A 1

B $\frac{9}{10}$

C $\frac{1}{5}$

D None of these

Answer [   ]

Q42 Two cards are drawn from a pack of 52. The first card is not returned before the second is drawn. What is the probability of the second card being a queen if the first was an ace of hearts?

A $^4/_{51}$

B $^4/_{663}$

C $^1/_{13}$

D $^4/_{52}$

Answer

Q43 What is the probability that the first two cards are not queens when drawn from a pack of 52 and the first card is not returned before the second is drawn? Express your answer on a probability scale of 1 to only two decimal points.

A 0.99

B 0.92

C 0.85

D 0.82

Answer

Q44 A restaurant chain's customer service department has calculated that the probability of a customer returning a meal as unsatisfactory is 0.005. If the average restaurant serves 500 people a day, what is the possibility that two consecutive customers will return their food (assume they are independent events).

A 0.005 + 0.005

B 0.005 × 0.005

C 0.005 divided by 500

D 0.005 × 600

Answer

Q45 In a restaurant belonging to the chain described in Q44, how many times a year would you expect two consecutive customers to return their food? Assume the restaurant is open most if not all days a year.

A   Between once and twice

B   Between two and three times

C   Between three and four times

D   Between four and five times

Answer

Q46 Find the mean of the following data:

150, 200, 250, 275, 300, 325

A   1,500

B   250

C   500

D   750

Answer

Q47 Find x minus the mean of x when the value of x is taken as 150.

x	$(x - \bar{x})$
150	
200	
250	
275	
300	
325	
Σx 1,500	

A   −100

B   −50

C   100

D   −75

Answer

Q48 Using a calculator and taking the value of x to be 150, find:

$(x - \bar{x})^2$

x	$(x - x)$	$(x - \bar{x})^2$
150	−100	
200	−50	
250	0	
275	25	
300	50	
325	75	

A 2,500

B 5,625

C 10,000

D 625

Answer [   ]

Q49 Again using a calculator, find:

$\Sigma(x - \bar{x})^2$

x	$(x - \bar{x})$	$(x - \bar{x})^2$
150	−100	10,000
200	−50	2,500
250	0	0
275	25	625
300	50	2,500
325	75	5,625

A 22,250

B 19,625

C 20,750

D 21,250

Answer [   ]

Q50 Find the standard deviation(s) for the following data using the formula and a calculator (only work each stage to one decimal place).

$$\sqrt{\frac{\Sigma(x - \bar{x})^2}{n}}$$

x	$(x - \bar{x})$	$(x - \bar{x})^2$
150	−100	10,000
200	−50	2,500
250	0	0
275	25	625
300	50	2,500
325	75	5,625

Σx 1,500 $\Sigma(x - \bar{x})^2$ = 21,250

A 15.7

B 49.3

C 59.5

D 75.2

Answer [   ]

End of test

Advanced numeracy

This chapter comprises two 50-question tests with question types that are typical of the advanced numerical tests currently in use. Both tests include examples of the following type of question: quantitative reasoning, data sufficiency, data interpretation and comprehension of quantitative terms. In each case the questions start off relatively easy.

These tests are intended as a source of reinforcement for the concepts and operations described elsewhere in this volume and its companion, *How to Pass Advanced Numeracy Tests* (revised edition Kogan Page, 2008). It is also intended that these tests will provide further valuable practice under realistic test conditions.

Answers and many explanations are provided on pages 212–19 and an interpretation of your score is provided on page 235–36.

You should only require a calculator to answer a few of these questions. Instead, practise at estimating and rounding sums to more convenient amounts. If you do resort to a calculator, use it in order to understand the operation better or to check your answer.

Test 6 Advanced numeracy test

Test instructions

This test comprises 50 questions. Allow yourself 40 minutes to complete it.

The test consists of a series of questions and labelled suggested answers to choose from. You are required to select one of the suggested answers as the correct one and to record that answer's identifying label in the answer box. This means that all questions will be answered by either A, B, C, D or E, depending on the number of suggested answers.

Attempt all questions in the allowed time and work without interruption or pause.

Do not turn the page until you are ready to begin the test.

Q1   Another word for an interpolation is:

A   Evaluation

B   Estimate

C   Non-linear

D   Relationship

Answer [   ]

Q2   A cube has a volume of 125cm^3. What is the length of one of its sides?

A   3cm

B   4cm

C   5cm

D   6cm

Answer [   ]

Q3   The term to indicate that an association exists between two quantities is:

A   Correspondent

B   Cross-tabulation

C   Description

D   Correlation

Answer [   ]

Q4   Which of the following is untrue of the reciprocal of x?

A   When multiplied by itself gives 1

B   Is $\dfrac{1}{x}$ or x^{-1}

C   When divided by itself gives 1

D   When x is a fraction its reciprocal is found by turning the fraction upside down

Answer [   ]

Q5 Is 161 a prime number?

A Yes

B No

Answer _____

Q6 The difference between the value obtained by sampling and the value if calcu-lated for the entire population is:

A Sampling error

B Sample limitation

C Sample range

D Sampling margin

Answer _____

Q7 A relationship between one item and another is called:

A Multiplier

B Ratio

C Coefficient

D Curve fitting

Answer _____

Q8 A set of data comprising all possible observations of an event is called:

A A population

B A sample

C A range

D None of these

Answer _____

Q9   What is the sum of the integers from 110 to 630?

    A   Under 200,000

    B   Between 200,000 and 220,000

    C   Between 220,000 and 240,000

    D   Over 300,000

Answer [   ]

Q10 A statistical population can be:

    A   Finite

    B   Infinite

    C   Both finite and infinite

    D   Either finite or infinite

Answer [   ]

Q11 What is the average of the inclusive integers from 162 through to 726?

    A   444

    B   564

    C   282

    D   432

Answer [   ]

Q12 Statistical sampling is:

    A   The process of selecting a representative sample

    B   An inference drawn from a representative sample

    C   A description of a representative sample's properties

    D   The study of methods by which data can be analysed

Answer [   ]

Q13 A ladder 8m long is resting against a wall so that the foot of the ladder is 3m from the wall. How far is the top of the ladder above the ground?

A 8.0m

B 7.8m

C 7.4m

D 7.0m

Answer

Q14 Quota sample means:

A A test to establish that a sales person has indeed reached his or her sales quota

B A method by which advertising executives establish the effectiveness of an advertising campaign

C The minimum number of members of a group who must be present for decisions or votes to be made

D A group of respondents who fulfil a researcher's quota classification

Answer

Q15 Quantitative research deals with:

A The transcripts of in-depth interviews

B Focus group reports

C Audience responses

D The number of audience members

Answer

Q16 XYZ is a triangle. Name the type of angle at Z if:

$$z^2 < x^2 + y^2$$

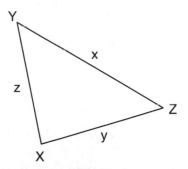

A   Right angle

B   Acute angle

C   Obtuse angle

D   Reflex angle

Answer

Q17 In forecasting, the term used to indicate the relative importance of an item is:

A   Value

B   Weight

C   Prediction

D   Sample

Answer

Q18 If a line joins two points with coordinates (a_1,b_1) and (a_2,b_2), what are the co-ordinates of the mid-point?

A $\dfrac{(a_1,b_1)}{(a_2,b_2)}$

B $\dfrac{(a_1,b_1,a_2,b_2)}{(\ 2 \quad 2\ )}$

C $\dfrac{(a_1,b_1) + (a_2,b_2)}{2}$

D $(a_1,b_1)^2 + (a_2,b_2)^2$

Answer

Q19 A graphic representation of a project's schedule is called:

A   Trendline chart

B   Project schedule

C   Gantt chart

D   Critical path

Answer [   ]

Q20 Check-in for a flight closes one hour before take-off. Which of the following statements is required to work out what time to leave for the airport?

A   The time of the flight

B   The time of the flight and the distance to the airport

C   The time of the flight and the average speed required to reach the airport before check-in closes

D   The check-in time and the time required to reach the airport before check-in closes

Answer [   ]

Q21 The square root of an integer for which the root is not exact is called:

A   An ioci

B   A cone

C   A surd

D   A sine

Answer [   ]

Q22 The compound interest for any year is interest paid on the total of the sum of money invested and the interest earned in previous years. The compound interest over several years is the total of the compound interest earned for every year. If an original amount is increased by J% to become a new amount, which of the following is correct?

A   This cannot be calculated without further information

B   The original amount = % original amount × the original amount as a decimal

C   The original amount = the new amount × $\dfrac{100 + J}{100}$

D   The original amount = the new amount $/\dfrac{100 + J}{100}$

Answer [   ]

Q23 Read the question and decide what combination of statements (1) and (2) is required to answer the question, if it can be answered.

In a horse race, Horse A and Horse B use different strategies to try to win the race. Which horse will be ahead at the end of the race?

(1)   Horse A covers the first half of the course 40 seconds faster than Horse B.
(2)   Horse B runs the second half of the race twice as quickly as Horse A.

There is sufficient information to be able to solve the question:

A   In (1) but not in (2)

B   In (2) but not in (1)

C   In (1) and (2) together

D   In (1) and (2) separately

E   In none of the statements

Answer [   ]

Q24 Read the question and decide what combination of statements (1) and (2) is required to answer the question, if it can be answered.

In a lottery, the third and fourth balls drawn are 12 and 27 respectively. What is the probability that the fifth ball drawn is number 7?

(1)   The lottery is drawn from a total of 50 balls numbered 1 to 50.
(2)   The first two numbers drawn are 4 and 28.

There is sufficient information to be able to solve the question:

A   In (1) but not in (2)

B   In (2) but not in (1)

C   In (1) and (2) together

D   In (1) and (2) separately

E   In none of the statements

Answer [   ]

Q25 Read the question and decide what combination of statements (1) and (2) is required to answer the question, if it can be answered.

A flight from London to New York leaves at exactly the same time as a flight from New York to London. Given that both flights cover exactly the same distance, is it possible to tell whether they will land at exactly the same time?

(1)   Both flights achieve exactly the same average speed.
(2)   The weight of both aircraft is exactly the same.

There is sufficient information to be able to solve the question:

A   In (1) but not in (2)

B   In (2) but not in (1)

C   In (1) and (2) together

D   In (1) and (2) separately

E   In none of the statements

Answer [   ]

Situation 1

Study the information provided in the charts and answer the questions that follow.

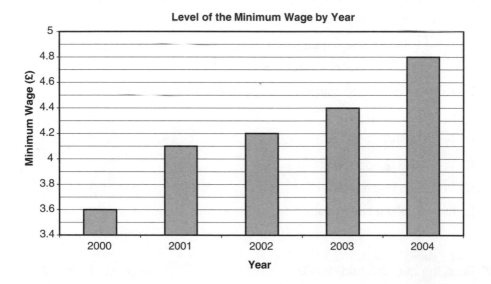

Level of the Minimum Wage by Year

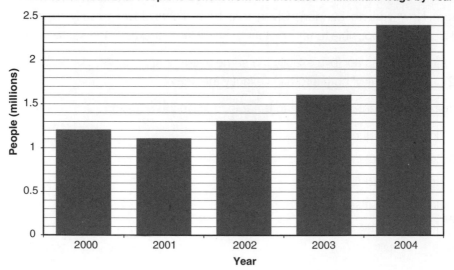

Number of Additional People to Benefit from the Increase in Minimum Wage by Year

The two charts above respectively illustrate the level of the minimum wage and the number of workers benefiting from an increase in the minimum wage over a five-year period. Use this information to answer the questions below.

Q26 Which year saw the lowest level of increase in the minimum wage?

    A 2000

    B 2001

    C 2002

    D 2003

    E 2004

Answer [   ]

Q27 What was the percentage increase in the minimum wage between 2000 and 2004? (Round your result to the nearest percentage point.)

    A 33%

    B 24%

    C 12%

    D 66%

Answer [   ]

Q28 How many people have benefited from the increases in the minimum wage between 2000 and 2004?

    A 2.3 million

    B 3.3 million

    C 6.7 million

    D 7.6 million

Answer [   ]

Situation 2

London offers a range of hotel accommodation to both tourists and business travellers. The graphs below present the number of hotels by star category found within the capital and the type of beds offered.

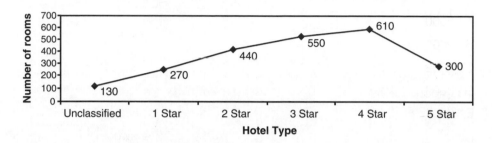

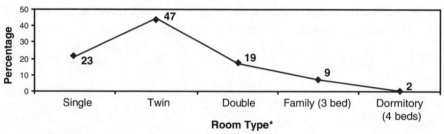

* as a percentage of all rooms in all types of hotel

Q29 How many hotels have fewer than 3 stars?

A   400

B   440

C   550

D   840

Answer

Q30 How many single rooms are there?

    A 529

    B 625

    C 1,250

    D 1,352

Answer [   ]

Q31 If every room was filled to capacity, how many people could sleep in the hotels in London?

    A 2,162

    B 4,370

    C 6,525

    D 8,566

Answer [   ]

Q32 20% of the twin rooms are found within the 3-star hotels. The tariff for these rooms is £65.00 per night. What is the total nightly revenue for this type of room at these hotels?

    A £3,360.00

    B £3,360.50

    C £3,560.30

    D £3,653.00

Answer [   ]

Situation 3

East Kirby has a very mixed economy and demonstrates variable employment rates. For 2002, the industrial occupancy and unemployment of both men and women were as follows:

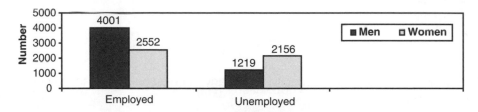

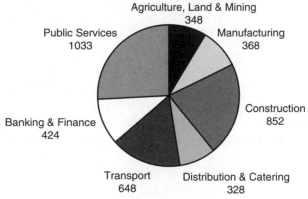

Occupation type: Men

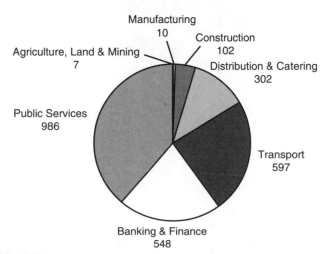

Occupation type: Women

Q33 How many more men than women live in East Kirby?

A   3,375

B   3,178

C   1,449

D   512

Answer _____

Q34 What percentage of the adult population is employed?

A   33%

B   50%

C   66%

D   75%

Answer _____

Q35 What percentage of the employed population work in the construction industry?

A   4%

B   9%

C   13%

D   14.5%

Answer _____

Q36 In which sector are more of the workers women than men?

A   Transport

B   Banking and finance

C   Distribution and catering

D   Public services

Answer _____

Q37 Complete the following sequence:

... 10, 15, 21, 28, 36, ??

A 43

B 44

C 45

D 46

Answer

Q38 If 10 is the fourth number in the sequence shown in Q37, what would the second number in this sequence be?

A 3

B 4

C 5

D 6

Answer

Q39 A bag contains five red balls and five blue balls. What is the probability that the first ball drawn is blue?

A .25

B .5

C .75

D 1

Answer

Q40 What is the correct equation to calculate the surface area of this shape?

A $2\pi r \times 2rh$

B $2rh^2/\pi$

C $(2\pi rh)^2$

D $2\pi r^2 + 2\pi rh$

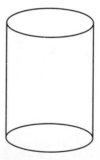

Answer

Q41 What is the volume of this shape? (All measurements in cm.)

A 648cm³
B 864cm³
C 216cm³
D 486cm³

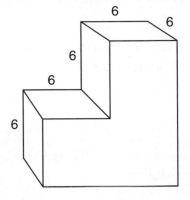

Answer

Q42 The following is a list of some quadrilaterals:

kite, parallelogram, rectangle, rhombus, square, trapezium.

Which quadrilaterals must have two pairs of equal sides?

A None
B All except the square
C All except the trapezium
D All except the rhombus

Answer

Q43 What is the simplified formula for the total perimeter of this shape?

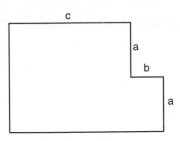

A $P = (a + b + c)^2$
B $P = 4a + 2b + 2c$
C $P = a^2 + 2b + 2c$
D $P = 2a + b + c$

Answer

Q44 The maximum speed, s km/hr, at which a Formula 1 racing car can race around a circular arc of racing track with a radius of r metres is given by:

$$s = x\sqrt{r}$$

When the radius is 100m, the maximum speed is 60 km/hr. What is the maximum speed when the radius is 300m?

A   96 km/hr

B   100 km/hr

C   104 km/hr

D   106 km/hr

Answer

Q45 Freddie Fashions is having a clearance sale on shirts. During the first week 50% reduction is offered, a further reduction of 10% off the original price is offered in week three and for the final week another 20% off the original price is offered in order to clear the stock. Jim bought a shirt on the very last day of the sale for £12.50. How much would it have cost before the sale?

A   £25.00

B   £50.00

C   £62.50

D   £65.00

Answer

Q46 Two dice are thrown. What is the probability that the sum of the faces is 5?

A $\frac{1}{5}$

B $\frac{1}{6}$

C $\frac{5}{6}$

D $\frac{1}{9}$

Answer

Q47 Eleven people were asked how many books they had read in the last year. These are their answers:

0, 2, 3, 3, 4, 5, 7, 8, 9, 11, 14

What is the mode of this set of answers?

A 3

B 2

C 6

D None of these

Answer

Q48 Using the set of data given in Q47, subtract the arithmetic mean value from the median value.

A 2

B 1

C 0

D −1

Answer

Q49 How many tiles sized 20cm by 30cm are required to tile a floor which is 4 metres by 4.5 metres?

A 100

B 200

C 300

D 400

Answer

Q50 What is the volume of a sphere with a radius of 3cm (treat π as 3.14)?

A 282.6cm^3

B 28.26cm^3

C 11.304cm^3

D 113.04cm^3

Answer

End of test

Test 7 Another advanced numeracy test

Test instructions

This test also comprises 50 questions, and again allow yourself 40 minutes to complete it.

The test consists of a series of questions and labelled suggested answers to choose from. You are required to select one of the suggested answers as the correct one and to record that answer's identifying label in the answer box. This means that all questions will be answered by either A, B, C, D or E, depending on the number of suggested answers.

Attempt all questions in the allowed time and work without interruption or pause.

Do not turn the page until you are ready to begin the test.

Q1   The arithmetic mean is obtained by:

A   Identifying the middle number

B   Moving the decimal point one place to the left

C   Dividing the sum of two or more items by the number of items

D   Identifying the value with the highest frequency

Answer [   ]

Q2   Find the mode of the data:

5, −1, −3, 4, −5, 1, 0, 1

A   1

B   There is not one

C   0

D   5

Answer [   ]

Q3   Imagine you toss a coin into the air and make a note of whether it lands heads or tails up. After 50 times you have noted the following:

Heads: 21 times
Tails: 29 times

If you continue to toss the coin a further 100 times, about how many times would you expect it to land heads up?

A   42

B   58

C   63

D   87

Answer [   ]

Q4 What is the maximum number of spheres with a radius of 10cm that you can fit into a cube of 8,000 cm^3?

A   1

B   2

C   3

D   4

Answer

Q5 Is 113 a prime number?

A   Yes

B   No

Answer

Q6 The first quartile:

A   Is the same as the median

B   Has three-quarters of the list above it

C   Has three-quarters of the list below it

D   Has a value the same as half of the interquartile range

Answer

Q7 What is the sum of all the integers from 96 through to 690?

A   Under 200,000

B   Between 200,000 and 250,000

C   Between 250,000 and 300,000

D   Over 300,000

Answer

Q8   Complete the sequence:

14, 15, 16, 18, 20, 21, 22, ??

A   23

B   24

C   25

D   26

Answer

Q9   Percentiles:

A   Are the same as quartiles

B   Are an unequal distribution across a statistical ranking

C   Comprise values that always add up to 100

D   Are a statistical ranking split into 100 equal parts

Answer

Q10 Identify the median of the data:

5, −1, −3, 4, −5, 1, 0, 1

A   0

B   1

C $^1/_2$

D $−^1/_2$

Answer

Q11 When the null hypothesis cannot be disproved, the researcher concludes that:

A   A perfect correlation between X and Y exists

B   A direct correlation between X and Y exists

C   The test must be rerun

D   No relationship exists between X and Y

Answer

Q12 Mixing syrup and alcohol in ratio 3:2 makes Cough Hard medicine. This can be purchased from the chemist in bottles holding 750ml. How much of this is syrup?

A 450ml

B 500ml

C 550ml

D 600ml

Answer [ ]

Q13 A shape is said to tessellate if it covers a surface without overlapping or gap. Which of the following will not tessellate?

A Hexagons

B Quadrilaterals

C Regular triangles

D Pentagons

Answer [ ]

Q14 If $\dfrac{p-q}{s} = \dfrac{p+s}{q}$ what is p in terms of the other letters?

A $s^2 + q^2$

B $(qs)^2$

C $q^2 - s^2$

D $\dfrac{q^2 + s^2}{q - s}$

Answer [ ]

Q15 Two or more quantities are in direct proportion if their ratio stays the same as the quantities increase or decrease. If two quantities, l and m, are in direct proportion, then which of the following is true?

A   When l = 0, m = 0

B   As one quantity halves, the other doubles

C   l is twice m

D   l is half m

Answer [＿＿＿＿＿]

Q16 If two lines are perpendicular, the product of their gradient is:

A   2

B   1

C   0

D   –1

Answer [＿＿＿＿＿]

Q17 In mathematics, subscripts are written:

A   In parentheses

B   Above the line

C   Below the line

D   In bold

Answer [＿＿＿＿＿]

Q18 x is an integer. What is the greatest value of x for which 2x < 9?

A   2

B   4

C   6

D   7

Answer [＿＿＿＿＿]

Q19 The formula $8x + 4y$ would give the total length of the sides of which shape?

    A Square-based pyramid

    B Cone

    C Cuboid

    D Cylinder

Answer _____

Q20 The expression $z^2y - zy^2$ can be factorized to what?

    A $(zy^2) - z$

    B z^2y^2

    C $zy(z - y)$

    D $2zy^2$

Answer _____

Study the information provided and answer the questions that follow.

Situation 1

The average tax bill for British households has increased with every budget announced by the Chancellor of the Exchequer. The increase between 1996/97 and 2003/04 for some usual household taxes is presented in the table below.

Type of Tax	1996/97 (£)	2003/04 (estimate £)
Income tax	2,800	5,180
National insurance	1,876	2,900
VAT	1,916	2,556
Fuel duty	696	1,014
Vehicle excise duty	172	190
Tobacco	308	408
Alcohol	232	312
Betting duty	60	48

Q21 How much more fuel duty did the usual British household pay in 2003/04?

A £842

B £318

C £100

D £80

Answer [   ]

Q22 What is the percentage decrease in betting duty?

A 34.5%

B 32.5%

C 20.0%

D 10.5%

Answer [   ]

Q23 How much more tax did a home owner who didn't smoke, drink or gamble pay in 2003/04?

   A £168

   B £2,347

   C £4,380

   D £4,548

Answer ┌─────────┐

Q24 If income tax is to increase at the same rate, what would the estimated income tax bill be in 2010/11?

   A £9,583

   B £8,953

   C £8,593

   D £8,539

Answer ┌─────────┐

Situation 2

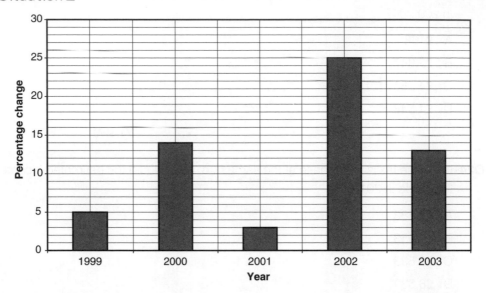

The above chart shows the percentage change in house prices between 1999 and 2003. Use this information to answer the questions below.

Q25 During which year was the increase in house prices the smallest, as indicated by the chart?

A 1999

B 2000

C 2001

D 2002

E 2003

Answer

Q26 Which year saw the fastest fall in the growth of house prices compared to the previous year?

A 1999

B 2000

C 2001

D 2002

E 2003

Answer

Q27 What was the mean rate of change in house prices over the five years shown?

A 10%

B 11%

C 12%

D 13%

E 14%

Answer

Q28 Using a straight trend line, estimate the theoretical level of rate of change in 2004 without taking any other considerations into account.

A Between 8% and 12%

B Between 13% and 16%

C Between 17% and 24%

D Between 25% and 29%

Answer

Situation 3

The residents of Oldcastle are a literary lot and love to read. The diagrams below indicate the age range of the population and the types of media read.

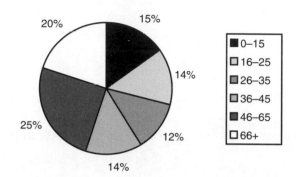

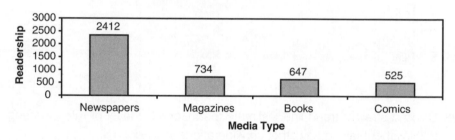

Q29 Assuming people only read one publication, how many more people read newspapers than books?

A 209

B 1,678

C 1,765

D 1,887

Answer

Q30 What is the greatest age range within the population?

    A 0–35

    B 16–35

    C 36–65

    D 46–66+

Answer [   ]

Q31 Which of the following is true?

    A 4,318 people live in Oldcastle

    B Magazines are read by 17% of the population

    C 17% of the people in Oldcastle read

    D Magazines account for 17% of the literature read

Answer [   ]

Q32 If the comics are read exclusively by 100% of the 0–15 year olds, what is the population of Oldcastle?

    A 3,481

    B 3,500

    C 4,318

    D 5,300

Answer [   ]

Q33 If a bag contains five red balls and five blue balls, and the first five balls drawn are all blue, what is the probability that the seventh ball drawn is red?

    A 1

    B .5

    C .25

    D .33

Answer [   ]

Q34 What is the area of an isosceles triangle that contains a right angle and two sides measuring 10cm?

A 30cm^2

B 50cm^2

C 40cm^2

D 33cm^2

Answer

Q35 Stochastic variables are:

A Predictable

B Sample selected

C Random

D Statistically descriptive

Answer

Q36 The Sun rises in the east. If you were able to look down on the Earth from over the North Pole, would it be rotating clockwise or anticlockwise?

A Anticlockwise

B Clockwise

C Impossible to tell

Answer

Q37 A decile is split into:

A 100 equal parts

B 1,000 equal parts

C 10 equal parts

D 5 equal parts

Answer

Q38 The weekly earnings of the workers at BIG Ltd have a mean of £240 and a standard deviation of £50. If the workers each receive a rise of £40 per week, what will be the new standard deviation?

A   £40

B   £50

C   £90

D   £280

Answer

Q39 A positive correlation is represented by:

A   A correlation coefficient greater than 0

B   A correlation coefficient less than 0

C   A scatter of points that lie in a straight line

D   A scatter of points that show a direct correlation

Answer

Q40 A bag contains 20 sweets, 10 of which are lemon and 10 vanilla flavoured. A sweet is drawn at random, and replaced, and a second is drawn at random. What are the chances (probability) that both sweets are lemon flavoured?

A $1/2$

B $1/4$

C $1/8$

D $1/16$

Answer

Q41 In the situation detailed in Q40, what are the chances that the first sweet is lemon flavoured but the second is vanilla?

A $1/2$

B $1/4$

C $1/8$

D $1/16$

Answer

Q42 With the same bag of sweets as in Q40, a sweet is drawn and returned to the bag, a second sweet is drawn and returned, and a third sweet is drawn and returned. What is the probability that all three are lemon?

A $1/8$

B $1/16$

C $1/4$

D $1/2$

Answer [   ]

Q43 $1m^2$ carpet tiles are bought in packs of six. A room to be fitted measures 18m × 5m. How many packs of tiles do I need to buy?

A 15

B 16

C 18

D 20

Answer [   ]

Q44 In statistics the meaning of range is:

A The sum of the values of a scatter of data

B The difference between the largest and smallest values

C The distance between the x coordinate and the value of the relevant data

D All the positive correlations subtracted from the negative correlations

Answer [   ]

Q45 At the local garden centre, pea canes have been delivered from the whole-salers in two batches. It was discovered that the first batch of canes measure 100.5cm, while the second batch measure 102.0cm in length. Given that the first batch is estimated to be the correct length, what is the relative error between the two batches?

A 1.0%

B 1.5%

C 2.0%

D 2.5%

Answer

Q46 A bag contains three balls, one red, one blue and one yellow. To the nearest percentage point, what is the percentage probability that the SECOND ball drawn will be yellow?

A 66%

B 100%

C 50%

D 33%

Answer

Q47 Another way to describe statistical sampling is:

A The null hypothesis

B Data sampling

C Simulation

D Representative sampling

Answer

Q48 What is the surface area of a box that is 3 metres long, 2 metres high and 2 metres deep?

A $64m^2$

B $32m^2$

C $27m^2$

D $125m^2$

Answer

Q49 Probability means:

A Anticipating problems

B Digitally encoding

C The likelihood of something happening

D The cumulative frequency of an event

Answer

Q50 Every hour the number of bacteria in a sample doubles. If the original number of bacteria is 100, and 50 bacteria are removed every two hours, how many bacteria are there after five hours?

A 3,050

B 3,900

C 1,900

D 2,700

Answer

End of test

Data interpretation

These tests are becoming extremely common and present you with a series of sets of data made up of, for example, a table, passage, graph or chart. The subject of the majority of these data sets will relate to the workplace and/or to business. However, expect the unexpected because the subjects are also drawn from every and any discipline. In some tests the amount of data presented is extensive and some is irrelevant, so you must filter through the material quickly to find the relevant items. Every set of data is followed by a series of questions each with a list of suggested answers. You have to sift through this information combining relevant data from the respective sources and select one of the suggested answers. In order to identify the correct answer you have to demonstrate good judgement and undertake calculations.

You are expected to answer the questions using only the information contained in the data set. Be careful if you know something on the subject or if you believe the data to be factually incorrect, controversial or out of date. It is not a test of your general knowledge, nor your knowledge of the last findings in the discipline or your political views. So feel completely at ease about answering a question using the data provided even if you believe it to be false, given what you have learned during your education or read in a newspaper that morning.

If you face a data interpretation test online or it is administered at a computer screen, be aware that diagrams on the screen can sometimes appear misleading, especially in the case of geometric shapes, tables and graphs as the screen in some instances can distort the image or the scale or both! The test author is aware of this and will have provided sufficient information to arrive at the answer. So if you are unlucky enough to find a distorted image or find its scale hard to read, rely on the written information and avoid drawing unnecessary assumptions about the appearance of a diagram, table or graph on the screen. For example, if a shape is described as a cube but on the screen the sides do not all seem equal, ignore the appearance of the sides and treat the shape as a cube. Equally, if a table or graph says that quantity x is the largest but on the screen it looks as if quantity y is the same or in fact bigger, take no notice and treat quantity x as the largest.

The following 60 practice questions are organized as two realistic practice tests. The tests provide a genuine test experience in terms of the question types, time allowed and the necessary sheer hard work and sustained concentration required of a real data interpretation test.

Test 8 Data interpretation

Test instructions

This test comprises 30 questions and you are allowed 40 minutes in which to complete it. There are a total of four sets of data. The first two are followed by five questions each and the next two are followed by 10 questions.

All questions are multiple choice. You are required to select one of the suggested answers labelled A–D as the correct answer and record its letter of the alphabet in the answer box. Q8 has suggested answers A–E.

To do well in this test you will have to avoid spending too long on any one of these questions and work quickly. You will also have to sustain a high level of concentration over the full 40 minutes.

You should be able to answer these questions without a calculator but use as much scrap paper as you wish.

Work without interruption.

Do not turn the page until you are ready to begin the test.

Data set 1

In 1995 it was estimated that 1 in 50 Britons now in their mid-80s would live to age 100 or older. This figure is a result of improved nutrition and medical treatment which has improved for 1 in 16 for people in their mid-80s now (in 2010). Official figures showed this estimate for 2000 to be 1 in 25.

There were 9,296 people aged 100 or over in Britain in 2008; an increase of 1,000 on 2007, according to the Office for National Statistics (ONS).

The findings come just a month after ONS data showed that there were 1.005 pensioners for every child under 16.

In recent years there have been seven women for every man who have lived to age 100 or older, but this ratio is declining as male life expectancy is improving at a faster rate than that of women. The number of centenarians has increased by 5.4% a year since 2008 and this trend is expected to continue for the next five or more years.

Q1   How many more Britons in a cohort of 100,000 in their mid-80s in 2010 can be expected to live to age 100 or older than a cohort of 100,000 Britons in their mid-80s in 1995?

A   6,250

B   5,750

C   5,000

D   4,250

Answer [   ]

Q2   How many more women than men were aged 100 or older in 2007?

A   1,037

B   6,222

C   7,259

D   8,296

Answer [   ]

Q3 In percentage terms what was the increase in the number of centenarians between 2007 and 2008?

A   Just over 12%

B   Between 10 and 12%

C   Above 5.4% but below 10%

D   5.4%

Answer

Q4 For every 100,000 children under the age of 16 how many more pensioners are there in 2010?

A   100,500

B   1,500

C   500

D   Cannot tell

Answer

Q5 Which of the suggested answers is the best estimate of the number of Britons in their mid-80s in 1995?

A   516,350

B   464,800

C   92,960

D   Cannot tell

Answer

Data set 2

Morning Tea

Market research findings relating to Morning Tea	
Market A	Market B
Competitor brands are winning Morning Tea's market share	Market leading brand
Price-sensitive market	Sold at a premium price
Customers base their decision to buy almost entirely on price	High level of customer loyalty (low level of brand switching)
Brand is sold at modest premium over competitors' brands	Customers perceive higher price to imply higher quality

Value of total sales of Morning Tea (000)				
Market A	$120	$120.304	$119	$119.696
Market B	$20	$19	$18	$19
	2005	2006	2007	2008

Units of Morning Tea sold into market A	
Year	(000)
2004	58.3
2005	80
2006	82.4
2007	92.7
2008	93.9

Q6 If Morning Tea was to be sold without a premium over competitors' products what would you expect to be the effect on the level of sales in the two markets?

A   Market A and B would both increase

B   Sales in market A would increase but B would remain the same

C   Sales in market B would decrease but A would show no change

D   Sales in market B would decrease but market A would increase

Answer [   ]

Q7 How many times bigger is market A than market B?

A   6.5

B   6.4

C   6.3

D   6.2

Answer [   ]

Q8 You were in a meeting with the finance director and he questioned one of the market research findings given below. Which one do you think he questioned?

A   Morning Tea is sold at a premium in market B

B   Competitor brands are winning Morning Tea's market share in market A

C   Market A is price sensitive

D   Market B is the market leading brand

E   Cannot tell

Answer [   ]

Q9 In market A for how much less did a unit of Morning Tea sell in 2006 compared with 2005?

A   2 cents

B   3 cents

C   4 cents

D   5 cents

Answer

Q10 In 2004 the unit value in market B was 30% that of market A. In the same year market A's unit price was 3% lower than its 2005 price. What was the value of sales for the two markets in 2004?

A $110,274.45

B $111,274.45

C $112,274.45

D $113,274.45

Answer

Data set 3

Training Unlimited

Training Unlimited has an annual international wage bill of $42,000,000 and an additional annual personal development budget of $1,260,000. Training Unlimited's 2,000 employees can select to attend personal development courses to a maximum value 5% of the average salary. They may choose from the following courses:

Public speaking*	$150	2 days
Effective e-mails	$475	1 day
Demonstrating leadership**	$350	3 days
Closing a sale*	$150	1 day
Dealing with conflict	$475	1 day
Personal safety	$150	1 day

Notes:
Employees can attend any course only once.
* These courses are open only to staff in sales positions.
** This course is open only to staff in managerial positions.
89% of Training Unlimited's staff are based in the USA.
60% of staff and associated costs shown relate to staff in sales positions.

Values	Annual total cost to training unlimited for all training in each module ($)
Public speaking	180,000
Effective e-mails	180,500
Demonstrating leadership	182,000
Closing a sale	180,000
Dealing with conflict	237,500
Personal safety	300,000
Total spend	1,260,000

Q11 What course, if any, did all Training Unlimited staff attend?

A   Public speaking

B   Effective e-mails

C   Dealing with conflict

D   Personal safety

Answer _____

Q12 How much more or less than 5% of the average wage is the training budget divided by the total number of employees?

A $420

B $540

C $590

D $630

Answer _____

Q13 How many working days were lost while staff attended the Effective e-mail module?

A   500

B   425

C   380

D   345

Answer _____

Q14 What total cost to Training Unlimited for sales staff is identified in the data set?

A $25,200,000

B $25,956,000

C $26,460,000

D $42,000,000

Answer _____

Q15 What percentage of the sales staff attended the Closing a sale module?

    A 100%

    B 90%

    C 80%

    D Cannot tell

Answer

Q16 What is the theoretical maximum number of days of training that a person in sales can attend?

    A 3

    B 4

    C 5

    D 6

Answer

Q17 One in four of the delegates who attended the demonstrating leadership module was a woman. What is this as a percentage of the total workforce?

    A 6.5%

    B 7%

    C 7.5%

    D 26%

Answer

Q18 How much more is it theoretically possible for a manager to spend on five days' training compared with a member of the sales team?

    A $450

    B $350

    C $150

    D $50

Answer

Q19 To what extent was the training budget spend in the year shown?

A   60%

B   100%

C   74%

D   87%

Answer _____

Q20 The Director of Human Resources must make proposals that will cut the personal development budget by 14.3% while ensuring the loss of the least possible number of days of training delivered. Which of the following suggestions will best meet these two objectives?

A   Removing the Effective e-mail module from the programme

B   Removing the Public speaking module from the programme

C   Negotiating a cut in the rates paid for all courses to a value of $180,000

D   None of the suggested answers

Answer _____

Data set 4

Lowest per capita income

Per capita income means how much every individual would receive in monetary terms if their country's yearly income was to be divided equally among everyone living there.

Per capita income 2009 ($)	
Mozambique	81
Ethiopia	123
Tanzania	155
Somalia	168
Nepal	179

Population (millions)	
Mozambique	$21^{1}/_{3}$
Ethiopia	79
Tanzania	$40^{1}/_{2}$
Somalia	$8^{1}/_{2}$
Nepal	28

Dollar millionaires

These are people with a net wealth of more than $1 million, excluding the value of primary residence and consumables. The number of millionaires around the world reached 10,249,998 last year (2009), up 6 per cent from the year before. All of the newcomers were from China, India and Brazil. There are reportedly over 80,000 dollar millionaires in India (the second fastest growth in the world behind Singapore). China has surpassed France and now stands fifth among the world for the number of its residents who qualify. China is reported to have 427,000 dollar millionaires (considerably more than France's 400,000).

Dollar a day labourers

A large number of people are landless and subsist on a $1 a day or less (in some cases a lot less). In many cases they are the only wage earner in an extended family.

Landless $1 a day or less labourers in 2009 (millions)	
Mozambique	9.6
Ethiopia	33.97
Tanzania	16.2
Somalia	4.675
Nepal	8.4

Q21 In 2008 how many dollar millionaires were there in the world?

    A 9,635,000

    B 9,669,800

    C 9,670,000

    D 9,671,800

Answer

Q22 What is the total $ difference between the countries with the highest and lowest yearly incomes?

    A 9,717,000

    B 8,864,000

    C 8,289,000

    D 5,012,000

Answer

Q23 Which percentage is the best estimate of the amount that the per capita income of Nepal is greater than that of Mozambique?

A 218%

B 219%

C 220%

D 221%

Answer

Q24 How much are the French dollar millionaires worth?

A 40,000 million

B 400,000 million

C 4,000,000 million

D Cannot tell

Answer

Q25 What percentage of Nepal's population is classed as dollar a day labourers?

A 29%

B 30%

C 31%

D 32%

Answer

Q26 In 2007 the yearly income of Tanzania was $4,440 million and the population was 3.5 million less than the population detailed in the table. By how much had the per capita income of Tanzania increased between 2007 and 2009?

A $35

B $34

C $33

D $32

Answer

Q27 How many dollar millionaires are there in Brazil?

A   73,198

B   73,138

C   72,842

D   Cannot tell

Answer

Q28 Which is best estimate of the fraction of the world's dollar millionaires in 2009 from China?

A $^1/_{26}$

B $^1/_{25}$

C $^1/_{24}$

D $^1/_{23}$

Answer

Q29 Which country has the highest percentage of dollar a day labourers?

A   Somalia

B   Mozambique

C   Tanzania

D   Nepal

Answer

Q30 The national debt of Mozambique is 5 times its total 2009 annual income. How much would each of China's dollar millionaires have to donate for that debt to be paid off?

A $20,234

B $20,118

C $19,876

D $19,340

Answer

End of test

Test 9 Another data interpretation test

This test also comprises 30 questions and you are again allowed 40 minutes in which to complete it.

There are a total of five sets of data. The first four are followed by five questions each and the last one is followed by 10 questions.

All questions are multiple choice. You are required to select one of the suggested answers labelled A–D as the correct answer, with two exceptions – Q16 has suggested answers A–F and Q19 has suggested answers A–E and you are required to select two of the suggested answers. You then record your answer's letter of the alphabet in the answer box.

To do well in this test you will have to avoid spending too long on any one of these questions and work quickly. You will also have to sustain a high level of concentration over the full 40 minutes.

You should be able to answer these questions without a calculator but use as much scrap paper as you wish.

Work without interruption.

Do not turn over the page until you are ready to begin the test.

Data set 1

Population growth

In 2008 the United Nations projected that by 2050 the world's population would increase by 37%. That same year (2008) the US population was found to be 305 million and growing. Half of the population were women.

The US population was projected to continue to grow until 2050 when it would reach 459.025 million, 60% of whom would be women, and make up 5.1% of the total world population. In 2008 the US Census Board found that people under 18 years of age made up 1/4 of the population and people 65 or more years of age represented 1/8 of the population. They also found that 80.8% of the population of the USA lived in urban centres and the most populous states were Texas and California. These trends are expected to continue to a point when in 2050, 28% of the population is expected to be resident in either the states of Texas or California.

Q1 In 2008 how many US residents living in an urban location were under 18 years old?

    A   184.83 million

    B   147.45 million

    C   123.22 million

    D   61.61 million

Answer [   ]

Q2 In 2008 how many US residents are aged 18–64?

    A   228,750,000

    B   190,625,000

    C   152,500,000

    D   114,375,000

Answer [   ]

Q3   In 2050 how many male US residents are predicted to reside in states other than Texas and California?

A   51,410,800

B   77,116,200

C   132,199,200

D   189,298,800

Answer

Q4   Between 2008 and 2050 by how many per cent is the US Census Board's prediction for the growth of the US population higher than the UN's prediction for the growth of the world population?

A   50.5%

B   37%

C   17.33%

D   13.5%

Answer

Q5   Which is the best estimation of the size of the world's population in 2008?

A   3.330 billion

B   4.405 billion

C   5.670 billion

D   6.570 billion

Answer

Data set 2

Worldwide.com

Worldwide.com has three production plants (No. 1) in Poland, (No. 2) in Bangladesh and (No. 3) in Mexico. Labour productivity figures are not yet available for the plant in Mexico but they are for those in Bangladesh (team A) and Poland (team B).

Labour productivity = output ÷ labour hours
Output = labour hours × units per hour per machine × number of machines
Capital productivity = output ÷ number of machines
Capacity utilization = output as a percentage of maximum production

Labour productivity		
Team	Labour hours	Units per hour per machine
A	120	50
B	144	45

Capital productivity	
Production plant	Number of machines
1	10
2	15
3	20

Q6 What is the difference between the output of the plants in Bangladesh and Poland?

A   25,200 units

B   90,000 units

C   82,000 units

D   22,200 units

Answer

Q7 What is difference between the capital productivity of the Bangladesh plant and the Poland plant?

A   840

B   6,000

C   6,480

D   480

Answer

Q8 What is difference between the labour productivity at the plants in Bangladesh and Poland?

A   325

B   300

C   675

D   1,075

Answer

Q9 The machines at the Bangladesh plant have a maximum production of 810 units. By how much would productivity at the Bangladesh plant have to improve if maximum production was to be achieved?

A   80%

B   24.75%

C   20%

D   8%

Answer

Q10 The capital productivity figure for Mexico at last arrives and is 2,760. What is the mean output for the production plants of worldwide.com?

A   67,000

B   68,000

C   71,000

D   70,000

Answer

Data set 3

Employment trends by region Latest job loss/gain by region (000)	
North	+33
North East	+70
North West	+172
South	−360
South East	−270
South West	−140
Negative = loss, positive = gain	

Previous total jobs by region (000,000)	
North	1.8
North East	1.4
North West	2.2
South	2.4
South East	1.6
South West	2.3

Latest unemployment by region (000)	
North	72
North East	49
North West	81.4
South	120
South East	39.9
South West	69

Previous unemployment by region (% change on latest)	
North	+4
North East	+3.5
North West	+3.7
South	−4.8
South East	−3.2
South West	−3
Negative = decrease, positive = increase	

Q11 In relative terms which Southern region saw the second largest variation (change) in jobs?

A   South

B   South East

C   South West

D   Cannot tell

Answer

Q12 Which region now has the second most jobs?

A   North West

B   South

C   North

D   South West

Answer

Q13 Which percentage most accurately expresses the latest level of unemployment in the South East region in relation to the latest number of jobs in that region?

A   33%

B   30%

C   23%

D   13%

Answer

Q14 Which statement can be deduced from the variation in jobs and employment in the North region?

A   On the whole the unemployed failed to access the increase in the number of jobs

B   The level of unemployment dropped because of the large number of jobs gained

C   The drop in the level of unemployment was modest relative to the number of jobs gained

D   The increase in jobs had minimal impact on unemployment

Answer [＿＿＿＿＿]

Q15 What is the new total number of jobs in the region where the job total increased by 12% of the total increase in jobs?

A   1,470,000

B   2,370,000

C   1,833,000

D   2,160,000

Answer [＿＿＿＿＿]

Data set 4

APS

Average propensity to save (APS) is a measure of a population's attitude towards saving money. In many instances APS is determined by culture. Some communities, for example in the Far East, place considerable importance on saving while others – examples include developed Western nations – do not. These cultural differences are reflected in wide differences in the APS of populations. Take for example, the population of the Punjab (population 5 in the table below) their APS is 0.7 and is among the highest in the world.

Population	Average saving $	Average income $
1	1,400	8,400
2	160	1,920
3	7,950	31,800
4	15,000	13,500
5	6,000	4,200
6	1,700	18,700

Q16 What is the APS for population 1 and is its propensity to save higher or lower than population 3? Select two letters from the suggested answers as the answer you believe correct. Select F if you do not believe the question can be answered on the information given.

A 6

B 7

C 1.66

D Higher

E Lower

F Cannot tell

Answer [　　　　　　　]

Q17 Which population would you estimate to place the least emphasis on the need to save?

A 6

B 3

C 2

D Cannot tell

Answer _____

Q18 Which of the suggested answers is the best estimation of the APS for populations 1, 2 and 5?

A 1.7

B 1.8

C 1.9

D 2.0

Answer _____

Q19 If the average savings for population 6 were to increase by $2,040 while income remained the same, by how much would the APS improve or worsen? (Indicate two letters from the suggested answers that you believe correct.)

A 6

B 5

C 4

D Improve

E Worsen

Answer _____

Q20 By how much would saving increase for population 3 if average income for that population was to increase to 39,750 while the APS remained the same?

A $9,937.5

B $1,987

C $1,987.5

D $7,950

Answer _____

Data set 5

Mary's Gums

Mary's Gums is a company that sells confectionery in the UK and Irish Republic. The managerial team's revenue targets are presented in the tables. Analyse them to answer the questions that follow.

Revenue 2006 ($000,000)	
Fruit Salad	1.2
Sour Cola	0.7
Cool Mints	2.4
Hard Gums	1.3
Soft Fruit	1.8

$ revenue growth targets for 2007	
Fruit Salad	24,000
Sour Cola	5,250
Cool Mints	72,000
Hard Gums	6,500
Soft Fruit	27,000

% annual revenue growth target for 2008	
Fruit Salad	3
Sour Cola	1
Cool Mints	4
Hard Gums	2.5
Soft Fruit	2

Q21 What will be the revenue generated from Cool Mints in 2007 if the target is missed by 15%?

A $24, 010,800

B $2,420,200

C $2,441,800

D $2,461,200

Answer [   ]

Q22 If all targets are realized what is the total revenue for the year 2007?

A $7,534,750

B $7,453,475

C $7,413,475

D $7,134,750

Answer [   ]

Q23 How much less is the percentage annual revenue growth target for Hard Gums in 2007 than 2008?

A   0.5%

B   2%

C   Double

D $3,250

Answer [   ]

Q24 What is the revenue growth target for Sour Cola and Soft Fruit as a percentage of the 2006 revenue?

A   1.29%

B   1.79%

C   2.29%

D   2.79%

Answer [   ]

Q25 Which of the following sources are likely to be of most help in estimating the potential market for Mary's Gums' products?

1	A report on the demography of the UK and Ireland
2	The annual accounts of Mary's Gums' rival confectioner
3	A trend survey on the spending habits of customers in the UK and Ireland's leading supermarket
4	A social economic profile of eaters of confectionery
5	A breakdown of sales by type of retail outlet in the UK and Ireland

A   4 and 3

B   5 and 2

C   3 and 1

D   1 and 4

Answer

Q26 By how much will the 2008 revenue for Sour Cola be below its target revenue for the three years, if the Sour Cola target for 2007 is missed by 2/3 but the 2008 target is realized?

A $3,500

B $7,035

C $7,000

D $3,535

Answer

Q27 Which one of the following four suggested strategies would both help evaluate the worth of current marketing activities and best realize the target growth for Cool Mints?

A   Suspend all marketing for a year to establish Cool Mints' true value in terms of the contribution to revenue

B   Decrease marketing expenditure slowly over two years to establish whether revenue decreases

C   Increase expenditure on marketing activities one by one to establish which activity, if any, leads to a rise in revenue

D   Increase marketing expenditure slowly over a year to see whether revenue increases

Answer [   ]

Q28 How much will the product Hard Gums generate in 2006 and 2007 combined, if the target during 2007 is exceeded by a factor of 20?

A $2,730,000

B $2,073,000

C $1,430,000

D $130,000

Answer [   ]

Q29 Which product's 2007 revenue growth target calculated as a percentage of its 2006 revenue is six times greater than the target for Hard Gums' 2007 revenue growth target calculated as a percentage of its 2006 revenue?

A   Fruit Salad

B   Sour Cola

C   Cool Mints

D   Soft Fruit

Answer [   ]

Q30 Which of the following statements are valid?

1	Over the three years shown Cool Mints is targeted to generate the most revenue.
2	The figures for Hard Gums in 2007 and 2008 combined give a target revenue increase of 3%.
3	Over the three years shown Sour Cola is targeted to generate the least revenue.
4	The figures for Fruit Salad in 2007 and 2008 combined give a target revenue increase of 3%.

A   All four statements are valid

B   Three of the four statements are valid

C   Two of the four statements are valid

D   Only one of the statements is valid

Answer

End of test

Answers and explanations

Test 1: Key quantitative operations

Q1

Fraction	Decimal	Percentage
$^3/_4$	0.75	75%
$^1/_5$	0.2	20%
$^3/_5$	0.6	60%
$^3/_8$	0.375	37.5%
$^1/_4$	0.25	25%

Q2 *Answer* C.
Explanation Simplifies to $^1/_4$, Highest Common Factor (HCF) is 8.

Q3 *Answer* C.
Explanation HCF is 22.

Q4 *Answer* A.
Explanation HCF is 6.

Q5 *Answer* B.
Explanation HCF is 13.

Q6   *Answer* D.
      Explanation $^3/_{12} + {}^8/_{12} = {}^{11}/_{12}$, which does not simplify any further.

Q7   *Answer* A.
      Explanation $^9/_{24} + {}^{20}/_{24} = {}^{29}/_{24} = 1^5/_{24}$.

Q8   *Answer* B.
      Explanation $^3/_6 + {}^1/_6 = {}^4/_6 = {}^2/_3$.

Q9   *Answer* D.
      Explanation $^4/_{12} - {}^3/_{12} = {}^1/_{12}$.

Q10 *Answer* B.
      Explanation $^{25}/_{30} - {}^9/_{30} = {}^{16}/_{30} = {}^8/_{15}$.

Q11 *Answer* C.
      Explanation Multiply the numerators and the denominators, which gives
      $^{10}/_{30} = {}^1/_3$, but you can simplify first, ie $^2/_5 \times {}^5/_6$ cancels out to $^1/_1 \times {}^1/_3 = {}^1/_3$.

Q12 *Answer* A.
      Explanation $^2/_7 \times {}^3/_4 = {}^6/_{28} = {}^3/_{14}$.

Q13 *Answer* C.
      Explanation A factor is a whole number that is a multiple without remainder.

Q14 *Answer* C.
      Explanation The factors of 12 are 1, 2, 3, 4, 6, 12. The factors of 18 are 1, 2, 3, 6, 9, 18. So the common factors are 1, 2, 3, 6.

Q15 *Answer* D.
      Explanation To multiply powers with the same base, add the powers.

Q16 *Answer* B.
      Explanation To divide powers with the same base value, subtract the powers.

Q17 *Answer* A.

Q18 *Answer* C.

Q19 *Answer* B.

Q20 *Answer* D.
      Explanation Suggested answer A gives the volume of a square, B the volume of a cylinder.

Q21 *Answer* D.
      Explanation 16 has more factors than 1 and itself. Its factors are 1, 2, 4, 8, 16.

Q22   *Answer* C.

Explanation   They are 1, 2, 4, 5, 10, 20.

Q23   *Answer* B.

Explanation   The base number must be multiplied by itself; then the sum of the first multiplication must be multiplied by the base number again. This must continue for as many times as the index value. The power of 2 sequence is as follows: 4, 8, 16, 32, 64, 128, 256, 512, 1,024.

Q24   *Answer* D.

Explanation   The values are: $2^7 = 128$, $3^5 = 243$, $15^2 = 225$, $6^4 = 1,296$.

Q25   *Answer* B.

Explanation   Suggested answer C is its value not its index form.

Q26   *Answer* A.

Explanation 8^2, 2^6, 4^3 all share the value 64, while the value of 6^2 is 36.

Q27   *Answer* B.

Explanation   The sequence is the first 5 square numbers.

Q28   *Answer* C.

Explanation   Square numbers are whole numbers. Learn to recognize the sequence of low value square numbers. $13 \times 13 = 169$.

Q29   *Answer* D.

Explanation $1.2 \times 1.2 = 1.44$.

Q30   *Answer* D.

Explanation $\sqrt{36} = 6$.

Q31   *Answer* B.

Explanation   Also learn to recognize the low value cubed numbers.

Q32   *Answers* A and D.

Explanation 1^3 and $1^2 = 1$; 4^3 and $8^2 = 64$.

Q33   *Answer* C.

Explanation   The answer given is 6^3 not 7^3.

Q34   *Answer* C.

Explanation $75\% = 0.75$; 0.75 of 32 = 24.

Q35   *Answer* B.

Explanation   This is a simple interest calculation so

$$1,000 + \frac{(1,000 \times 3 \times 5)}{100} = 1,150.$$

Q36 *Answer* B.
Explanation $1,000 \times (1 + \frac{3}{100})^5$.

Q37 *Answer* C.
Explanation $3^2 + 4^2 = C^2$; $9 + 16 = 25$; $\sqrt{25} = 5$.

Q38 *Answer* A.
Explanation $^4/_3 \times 3.14 \times 3^3$.

Q39 *Answer* C.
Explanation $3.14 \times 3^2 \times 5 = 3.14 \times 9 \times 5 = 141.3\text{cm}^3$.

Q40 *Answer* D.
Explanation $2\pi2^2 + \pi \times 2 \times 2 \times 4 = 25.12 + 50.24 = 75.36\text{cm}^2$.

Q41 *Answer* C.

Q42 *Answer* A.

Q43 *Answer* C.
Explanation $x = 4$, $y = 3$, $z = 14$; $\Sigma xyz = 21$.

Q44 *Answer* A.

Q45 *Answer* D.
Explanation Apply the square root to both sides.

Q46 *Answer* B.

Q47 *Answer* C.
Explanation Look carefully at the y scale.

Q48 *Answer* A.

Q49 *Answer* D.

Q50 *Answer* C.
Explanation Remember that a negative if squared becomes positive.

Q51 *Answer* D.
Explanation You can see that the curve is the same as in the previous question only it has shifted to the left by one on the x scale.

Q52 *Answer* B.
Explanation < means less than so x could be any value less than 4 (so not 4).

Q53 *Answer* A.
Explanation ≥ means more than or equal to so x could be any value 3 or above.

Q54 *Answer* C.
Explanation 16 is less than 20.

Q55 *Answer* B.
Explanation The symbol always points to the smaller value.

Q56 *Answer* D.
Explanation x is any value less than −2.

Q57 *Answer* C.

Q58 *Answer* B.
Explanation Solid lines indicate ≤ ≥; < > are indicated with broken lines.

Q59 *Answer* A.
Explanation Substitute y = 0 and x = 0 into the equation. If it is untrue then the shaded area is opposite the 0,0 point.

Q60 *Answer* A.
Explanation 84 divided by 6 = 14.

Q61 *Answer* B.
Explanation $\dfrac{(13 \times 2) + (14 \times 3) + (15 \times 6) + 16}{12} = {}^{174}/_{12} = 14.5$

Q62 *Answer* C.
Explanation The modal value is simply the most frequent value.

Q63 *Answer* A.
Explanation To find the median, arrange the data into numerical order and take the middle value.

Q64 *Answer* C.
Explanation The range is obtained by subtracting the lowest value from the highest.

Q65 *Answer* C.
Explanation The cumulative frequency is given so the answer can be simply taken from the table.

Q66 *Answer* D.
Explanation 18:63 cancels to 2:7.

Q67 *Answer* C.
Explanation The lowest terms for 20:60 are 1:3.

Q68 *Answer* D.

Explanation   The ratio comprises 9 parts (3 + 2 + 4). 270 divided by 9 = 30, so:

Institution 1: 30 × 3;

Institution 2: 30 × 2;

Institution 3: 30 × 4.

Q69 *Answer* D.

Explanation   120 = 100%; $^{120}/_{100}$ = 1%, so 1.2 = 1%; $\dfrac{30}{1.2}$ = 25%.

Q70 *Answer* B.

Explanation $^{360}/_{100}$ = 3.6 × 6 = 21.6.

Q71 *Answer* B.

Explanation   1.04 × 8 = 8.32.

Test 2: Fundamental accounting terms

Q1   *Answer* A.

Explanation   The fact that the depreciation is accelerated suggests that the amount deducted cannot be equal or represented by a straight line.

Q2   *Answer* B.

Explanation   Accounts payable are the sums owed to a supplier. They do not include salaries or bank or director loans etc.

Q3   *Answer* A.

Q4   *Answer* B.

Explanation   Apportionment involves apportioning or allocating items to headings. It can be done by agreed formula or by item. In the case of the latter, this is the direct method.

Q5   *Answer* C.

Explanation   Suggested answer C would appear on a statement of profit and loss.

Q6   *Answer* C.

Explanation   In business, an accounting year can begin and end on any day but often it coincides with either the calendar year or fiscal year (tax year end). Dividends if paid are often announced at or near a company's year end but not necessarily on any particular date.

Q7   *Answer* B.

Explanation   Trial balances are an accounting tool used in the production of year-end accounts.

Q8   *Answer* D.

Explanation   Single entry bookkeeping is an incomplete method of recording the finances of a business whereby all transactions are recorded in one account.

Q9   *Answer* A.

Q10   *Answer* C.

Explanation   An operating profit or loss is the gross margin and includes the cost of normal business overheads only.

Q11   *Answer* C.

Explanation   Be confident about the difference between net and gross. The value of someone's assets would have to be the gross worth where any liabilities have to be deducted to establish the net value. A person's salary after tax and other deductions is the person's net income.

Q12   *Answer* C.

Q13   *Answer* B.

Q14   *Answer* A.

Q15   *Answer* D.

Explanation   Force majeure is something that causes an unavoidable delay.

Q16   *Answer* B.

Explanation   Disbursements service debts while distributions share profits or earnings. A debt is only discharged when it is fully paid.

Q17   *Answer* A.

Q18   *Answer* C.

Explanation   Suggested answer B would involve writing the balance off.

Q19   *Answer* D.

Q20   *Answer* D.

Q21   *Answer* D.

Q22   *Answer* C.

Q23   *Answer* B.

Q24   *Answer* C.

Q25   *Answer* C.
   Explanation   A fixed cost does not change with the level of production.

Q26   *Answer* C.
   Explanation   Equity is assets minus liabilities so it is also net worth.

Q27   *Answer* D.
   Explanation   Earned income is from services provided by the person.

Q28   *Answer* B.

Q29   *Answer* A.
   Explanation   A debit is a debt that occurs on the left-hand side of the account.

Q30   *Answer* B.
   Explanation   A credit is on the right-hand side of the account.

Q31   *Answer* D.
   Explanation   After direct cost of sales, all other costs are deducted to produce net profit or profit before tax.

Q32   *Answer* A.
   Explanation   A cost in this sense is an asset because the item acquired retains a value.

Q33   *Answer* D.

Test 3: Business comprehension

Q1   *Answer* D.
   Explanation   A liability without limit or fault could result with or without negligence or an intentional act. It may be shared or fall solely to one person, so D is correct.

Q2   *Answer* A.
   Explanation   These are increases in costs that do not lead to an increase in the charge of a service or product, so they are absorbed by the business.

Q3   *Answer* C.
   Explanation   In accounting terms the actual cost is the amount paid irrespective of costs incurred in the purchase or its subsequent value.

Q4   *Answer* D.

Q5   *Answer* D.

Explanation   A conglomerate is the product of agglomeration, the bringing together of diverse commercial entities into a single organization. Suggested answer C sometimes results if the holding company's management are not familiar with all the group's areas of business.

Q6   *Answer* A.

Explanation   Total output is a key concept in macroeconomics, which is concerned with whole economies. Suggested answer D is the corresponding concept, total demand.

Q7   *Answer* B.

Explanation   To amortize a loan is to pay it off, at least in part, by a series of payments.

Q8   *Answer* D.

Explanation   These products are normally purchased by people on their retirement with the funds from their pension fund.

Q9   *Answer* A.

Explanation   Suggested answer C could be an example of appropriated expenditure, but its definition is a sum set aside for a particular expenditure or purpose.

Q10   *Answer* C.

Explanation   An asset may bring a return or be used to secure a loan but it is simply something owned with a value.

Q11   *Answer* A.

Q12   *Answer* D.

Explanation   A bond may or may not pay interest and some may provide tax-free income but they imply an obligation to pay.

Q13   *Answer* A.

Explanation   A yield can be produced by an investment other than one that is a business deal, for example the yield to government from a new tax. A yield can be expressed as a rate or a percentage, but neither mean yield.

Q14   *Answer* B.

Q15   *Answer* A.

Explanation   A hierarchically structured organization may be bureaucratic but it is not always the case.

Q16 *Answer* C.

Q17 *Answer* D.

Q18 *Answer* D.

Q19 *Answer* A.
Explanation   The system is widely used in research and market analysis to class all types of economic activity.

Q20 *Answer* D.
Explanation   Raising prices might ensure that profits are maintained but it would not stabilize a market. The other suggestions are used by governments in an attempt to stabilize for example currency and labour markets.

Q21 *Answer* C.

Q22 *Answer* B.

Q23 *Answer* A.

Q24 *Answer* C.

Q25 *Answer* A.
Explanation   'Seed money' is a term used widely by venture capitalists and relates to the first contribution they make to a start-up business.

Q26 *Answer* D.

Q27 *Answer* C.
Explanation   A royalty is earned so as long as the product is an intellectual one such as a literary work or computer program.

Q28 *Answer* B.
Explanation   In this context underwriting is provided by an investment bank to protect against losses during the issue period.

Q29 *Answer* A.
Explanation   Revenue is earnings before the cost of sales. It is also governmental tax receipts.

Q30 *Answer* D.
Explanation   A covenant is a contractual agreement to do or not do something.

Q31   *Answer* B.

Explanation   Verbal contracts are just as binding as written ones. They are simply harder to enforce because of the possible lack of evidence of the terms of the contract. Notice would only avoid a risk of penalty if the contract allowed for this.

Q32   *Answer* C.

Q33   *Answer* A.

Explanation   In financial markets a rally means that widespread increases in prices are occurring.

Q34   *Answer* A.

Explanation   Quality assurance is a management method that seeks total quality and zero defects. The meeting of groups of employees to discuss quality is called 'quality circles'.

Q35   *Answer* B.

Q36   *Answer* D.

Q37   *Answer* C.

Explanation   It is generally held that the higher the risk the higher the return so the relationship is a positive correlation.

Q38   *Answer* C.

Explanation   This term occurs in the technical press when it covers predatory takeover bids.

Q39   *Answer* D.

Explanation   The term 'petrodollars' refers to the funds invested in Western banks, and for a number of decades was key to understanding international economies.

Q40   *Answer* A.

Q41   *Answer* B.

Q42   *Answer* D.

Explanation   These loans are for large sums so the banks spread them across a number of participating institutions. One lender takes the lead in the administration of the loan.

Q43   *Answer* C.

Explanation   The law rules that it is for management to work constantly towards avoiding the natural state of inactivity towards which all businesses are heading.

Q44 *Answer* B.
Explanation   An example was when people stopped going to local shops and bought their goods in supermarkets instead. A move from competition to monopoly would be an example of a paradigm shift but is not the meaning of the term.

Q45 *Answer* A.

Q46 *Answer* B.

Q47 *Answer* B.

Q48 *Answer* A.
Explanation   Negative amortization results when the amount owed increases despite repayments. It might occur when for example the repayments are fixed at a particular rate but the interest increases to such an extent that the repayments fail to meet the interest charges.

Q49 *Answer* B.

Q50 *Answer* A.

Q51 *Answer* C.

Q52 *Answer* D.

Q53 *Answer* D.

Q54 *Answer* C.
Explanation   It is also a method of inventory costing.

Q55 *Answer* C.

Q56 *Answer* B.

Q57 *Answer* B.

Q58 *Answer* D.
Explanation   The line forms a J shape. Kondratieff was the economist who described supercycles of growth and recession.

Q59 *Answer* C.

Q60 *Answer* A.
Explanation   Pull inflation occurs when there are too few goods to meet demand. Suggested answers C and D are examples of pull accounting.

Q61 *Answer* C.
Explanation   Demand for luxury goods is considered highly elastic because changes in price greatly affect demand.

Q62 *Answer* D.

Explanation   A machine for example as it ages costs more to maintain so the surplus income it generates falls. When the surplus income falls below the operating cost the item is said to have reached the end of its economic life.

Q63 *Answer* B.

Q64 *Answer* C.

Explanation   A Dutch auction is used when for example a company wants to realize a lower unit price from its suppliers. Bids would begin at the current unit price and the suppliers would bid downwards to become the sole or preferred supplier at a much reduced profit margin.

Q65 *Answer* A.

Explanation   Suggested answer D is the modal value.

Q66 *Answer* C.

Explanation   An example might be the head office, accounts section or personnel department.

Q67 *Answer* B.

Explanation   They are traded on commodity exchanges.

Q68 *Answer* A.

Q69 *Answer* C.

Q70 *Answer* C.

Explanation   Junior shares are in some way restricted with for example no voting rights.

Q71 *Answer* C.

Q72 *Answer* B.

Explanation   Suggested answer A would represent an operating risk not one to an inventory.

Q73 *Answer* D.

Q74 *Answer* A.

Q75 *Answer* C.

Explanation   They are issued by banks and governments and guarantee payment.

Q76   *Answer* A.

Explanation   This widely adopted standard is managed by the International Organization for Standardization.

Q77   *Answer* B.

Q78   *Answer* D.

Q79   *Answer* A.

Q80   *Answer* D.

Q81   *Answer* A.

Q82   *Answer* B.

Explanation   These taxes are levied on particular goods or services.

Q83   *Answer* A.

Q84   *Answer* B.

Q85   *Answer* C.

Q86   *Answer* C.

Q87   *Answer* B.

Q88   *Answer* C.

Explanation   Supermarket own brands are an example of generic products.

Q89   *Answer* D.

Explanation   Suggested answer A is golden handcuffs, B golden hello and C a bonus. A golden parachute compensates for losing a job when perhaps a company is sold.

Q90   *Answer* A.

Explanation   When you have a poor return on an activity you incur a high opportunity cost because you have failed to take up possibly more profitable alternatives.

Q91   *Answer* C.

Explanation   This is a product produced exclusively by the owner of the patent or copyright.

Q92   *Answer* A.

Explanation   Brown goods are household electronic goods. Household electrical goods such as washing machines, freezers etc are white goods.

Q93   *Answer* C.

   Explanation   It involves selling goods or services, for example computer, printer and software, together as a discounted package.

Q94   *Answer* D.

   Explanation   The takeover integrates the commercial process.

Q95   *Answer* B.

   Explanation   The idea is to push the product into the market place. Advertising is used in a pull strategy where customer demand pulls the product into the market place.

Test 4: A test of geometry

Q1   *Answer* A.

Q2   *Answer* B.

   Explanation   The triangle is an equilateral triangle, which has equal sides, so must also have three equal angles that add up to 180°.

Q3   *Answer* D.

   Explanation $4^3 = 64$.

Q4   *Answer* C.

   Explanation   Angles CDB and DCB are given. So DBC = 180 − 90 − 25 = 65°; ABD can now be found = 180 − 65 = 115°; now x can be found, x = 180 − 45 − 115 = 20°.

Q5   *Answer* D.

   Explanation   In an isosceles triangle the two marked sides are equal as are the two base angles.

Q6   *Answer* A.

   Explanation   Divide the kite into two isosceles triangles.

Q7   *Answer* C.

   Explanation   Vertically opposite angles are equal when straight lines intersect. So x + 70 = 180, so x = 110; x + y = 180, so y also = 70.

Q8   *Answer* B.

   Explanation   A rule worth remembering is that the sum of two sides of any triangle must be more than the value of the remaining side; otherwise it cannot be constructed.

Q9   *Answer* A.
Explanation   x corresponds to the angle alongside the given angle,
so x + 70 = 180, so x = 110°.

Q10   *Answer* B.
Explanation   The smallest angle is always opposite the smallest side,
namely AC.

Q11   *Answer* C.
Explanation   All sides and angles of a regular polygon are equal and the
interior angles total 180°.

Q12   *Answer* A.
Explanation   The exterior angles of a regular polygon = 360°.

Q13   *Answer* D.
Explanation   The interior angles of a triangle = 180° so a pentagon
= 3 × 180 = 540°.

Q14   *Answer* C.
Explanation   A hexagon is a regular polygon with six sides so $^{360}/_6 = 60°$.

Q15   *Answer* D.
Explanation   A quadrilateral has four sides. Another example is the kite.

Q16   *Answer* D.
Explanation   A pentagon is a five-sided polygon and an octagon is an eight-
sided polygon. They can be divided as follows:

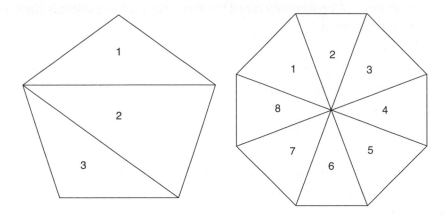

Q17   *Answer* D.
   Explanation   Circumference $= 2\pi r = 2 \times 3.14 \times 5 = 31.4$.

Q18   *Answer* B.
   Explanation $C = \pi d$.

Q19   *Answer* D.
   Explanation $31.4 = 3.14 \times 2 \times X$; $\frac{31.4}{3.14} = 10$; $\frac{10}{2} = 5$.

Q20   *Answer* C.
   Explanation   Area of a circle $= \pi r^2 = 3 \times 3 \times 3.14 = 28.26$.

Q21   *Answer* A.
   Explanation $r = \frac{1}{2}d$; $3.14\, r^2 = 3.14 \times 5 \times 5 = 78.5$.

Q22   *Answer* C.
   Explanation $C = 2\pi r$; $25.12 = 2\pi r$; $r = \frac{25.12}{6.28} = 4$.
   Area $= \pi r^2 = 3.14 \times 16 = 50.24$.

Q23   *Answer* B.
   Explanation $C = \pi d$; $d = \frac{21}{3} = 7$; $r = \frac{d}{2} = 3.5$.
   Area $= \pi r^2$; $r^2 = 12.25$; $12.25 \times 3 = 36.75$.

Q24   *Answer* D.
   Explanation   Volume $= \frac{4}{3}\pi r^3$, $r^3 = 27$, $\frac{4}{3} \times 3.14 \times 27 =$
   $$\frac{4 \times 3.14 \times 27}{3} = 113.04.$$

Q25   *Answer* C.
   Explanation   A hemisphere is half a sphere. So it is the same calculation as
   for Q24 divided by 2.

Q26   *Answer* C.
   Explanation   The shape comprises 3 identical surfaces, each of which
   occurs twice. So surface area $= 2(2 \times 3 + 5 \times 3 + 2 \times 5)$.

Q27   *Answer* A.
   Explanation   Area $=$ length $\times$ breadth $\times$ height.

Q28   *Answer* D.
   Explanation $60m = 60{,}000mm$; $v = \pi r^2 h = 3.14 \times 144 \times 60{,}000 =$
   $27{,}129{,}600mm^3 = 27{,}129.6m^3$.

Q29   *Answer* B.
   Explanation   Area $= \frac{36}{360} \times \pi r^2 = 0.1 \times 3.14 \times 9 = 2.826cm^2$.

Q30 *Answer* D.
Explanation   Arc = $^{72}/_{360}$ × 2πr = 0.2 × 31.4 = 6.28.

Q31 *Answer* C.
Explanation   Surface area = 2πr² + 2πrh = 157 + 188.4.

Q32 *Answer* A.
Explanation   The diagram illustrates well Pythagoras' theorem so
x = 9cm² + 25cm² = 34cm².

Q33 *Answer* B.
Explanation   The hypotenuse is the sloping side of the triangle. The square
of its length = the sum of the square of the other two sides, so length of
H = $\sqrt{25}$ = 5.

Q34 *Answer* D.
Explanation   x² = 10² – 8² = 100 – 64 = 36; $\sqrt{36}$ = 6cm.

Q35 *Answer* D.
Explanation   A right-angled triangle can be drawn on the grid with sides
3cm and 4cm in length, so length of line x = 3² + 4² = 9 + 16 = 25; $\sqrt{25}$ = 5.

Q36 *Answer* C.
Explanation   If plotted the points would give a line on which a right-angled
triangle can be drawn with sides 5cm and 12cm. So distance between
points squared = 5² + 12² = 25 + 144 = 169; distance = $\sqrt{169}$ = 13cm.

Q37 *Answer* B.
Explanation   To get the circumference you need either the radius or
diameter. The hypotenuse of the right-angled triangle is the length of the
diameter so: c = πd; diameter squared = 4² + 6² = 16 + 36 = 52;
d = $\sqrt{52}$ = 7.21; c = 3.14 × 7.21 = 22.63.

Q38 *Answer* A.
Explanation   26² = 24² + 10².

Q39 *Answer* C.
Explanation   Tan a = $\dfrac{\text{opposite}}{\text{adjacent}}$
So x = tan a × 8.

Q40 *Answer* A.
Explanation   Sin a = $\dfrac{\text{opposite}}{\text{hypotenuse}}$
So sin a = $^{8}/_{x}$.

Q41 *Answer* B.

Explanation   To find an angle from its cosine use the cos^{-1} function on a calculator.

$$\text{Cos } a = \frac{\text{adjacent}}{\text{hypotenuse}}$$

Cos $a = {}^{7}/_{11}$; size of a = cosine $a^{-1}\,{}^{7}/_{11}$.

Q42 *Answer* C.

Explanation   Sin 30 = o/h 0.5 = 3/h so h = 6cm.

Q43 *Answer* A.

Explanation   Cos 30 = y/6; 0.866 = y/6; 0.866 × 6 = y.

Q44 *Answer* D.

Explanation   Sin 66.6 = ${}^{138}/_{x}$; 0.917 = ${}^{138}/_{x}$; 0.917 × x = 138; x = ${}^{138}/_{.917}$. Diameter of semicircle = 150.49; circumference of semicircle = $\frac{1}{2}\pi d$ + d = 236.269 + 150.49 = 387 (nearest whole cm).

Q45 *Answer* A.

Explanation   Sin 1 = 90° so the triangles are right angled. To find the length of the diameter we use the sine ratio (sin angle = o/h). Sin .5 = 30; $\sqrt{27.04}$ = 5.2. .5 = ${}^{x}/_{5.2}$; .5 × 5.2 = 2.6cm.

c = πd; c = 3.14 × 2.6 = 8.164.

Q46 *Answer* A.

Explanation   Draw the plane on the diagram and you form a right-angled triangle of which you are given the lengths of two sides. From this you can calculate F,A,B. So tan angle FAB = ${}^{18}/_{32.5}$, so tan angle = ${}^{18}/_{32.5}$ = 0.55385 = 29°.

Q47 *Answer* D.

Explanation   We need to know AC and can find it using Pythagoras' theorem. AC^2 = 32.5^2 + 25^2 = 1,056.25 + 625 = 1,681.25; $\sqrt{1,681.25}$ = 41cm. Again using Pythagoras' theorem we can now find AG.

AG^2 = AC^2 + CG^2.

AG^2 = 1681.25 + 324 = 2005.25; AG = $\sqrt{2005.25}$ = 44.78 (to two decimal places).

Q48 *Answer* A.

Explanation   Plot the relative positions and you realize a right-angled triangle is formed. Use Pythagoras' theorem to calculate the length of BC. 4^2 + 3^2 = BC^2, 16 + 9 = 25; BC = $\sqrt{25}$ = 5.

Q49 *Answer* B.

Explanation   The basic sin, cos, tan ratios can only be used with right-angled triangles. We will only be able to answer this if we now use the cosine rule, which states:

$a^2 = b^2 + c^2 - 2bc \cos A$;

$a^2 = 16 + 25 - 2 \times 20 \times \cos A$;

$a^2 = 41 - 40 \times .5$;

$a^2 = 21$;

$a = 4.58$ (answer to two decimal points).

Q50 *Answer* C.

Explanation   The cosine of 100 is a negative. Again use the cosine rule:

$a^2 = b^2 + c^2 - 2bc \cos A$:

$a^2 = 49 + 81 - 2 \times (7 \times 9) \times -0.173$;

$a^2 = 49 + 81 - 126 \times -0.173$;

$a^2 = 49 + 81 - -21.798$;

$a^2 = 151.798$ (two negatives = a positive);

$a = 12.32$ (to two decimal places);

Perimeter = $9 + 7 + 12.32 = 28.32$.

Test 5: A further test of quantitative operations

Q1   *Answer* C.

Explanation   3 divided by 8 × 100 = 37.5.

Q2   *Answer* A.

Explanation   Convert the ratios to fractions ($\frac{1}{9}$, $\frac{3}{9}$, $\frac{5}{9}$) and then to percentages.

Q3   *Answer* B.

Explanation   5 divided by 16 × 100 = 31.2.

Q4   *Answer* D.

Explanation   4 divided into 7 × 100 = 57.1 (to one decimal point).

Q5   *Answer* A.

Explanation $\sqrt{23} = 4.79$. Prime numbers to 4.79 = 2, 3, neither of which divides exactly into 23, so 23 is a prime number.

Q6   *Answer* C.

Q7   *Answer* C.

Q8   *Answer* A.

Q9   *Answer* A.
Explanation $\sqrt{19}$ = 4.35. Prime numbers to 4.35 = 2, 3, neither of which divides exactly, so 19 is a prime number.

Q10   *Answer* A.
Explanation $^{50}/_{150}$ = $^1/_3$ × 100 = 33 (expressed as nearest whole percentage point).

Q11   *Answer* C.

Q12   *Answer* B.
Explanation   938 divided by 7 × 6 = 804.

Q13   *Answer* D.

Q14   *Answer* B.
Explanation   2 and 3 for example both divide into 222, so 222 is not a prime number.

Q15   *Answer* B.
Explanation $^5/_{16}$, $^5/_{16}$, $^6/_{16}$; then into percentages, eg 5 divided into 16 × 100.

Q16   *Answer* C.
Explanation   20 = $^1/_{300}$ × the number, so 20 = $^1/_3$ of 1% of 6,000.

Q17   *Answer* B.
Explanation   £10,000 – 20% = £8,000 – 30% = £5,600 – 40% = £3,360.

Q18   *Answer* D.
Explanation $\dfrac{16,000}{103.6} \times 100$

Q19   *Answer* A.
Explanation   Square root of 337 is 18.35. Prime numbers to value of 18.35 = 2, 3, 5, 7, 11, 13, 17. None divide exactly into 337, so 337 is a prime number.

Q20   *Answer* B.
Explanation   84% (100 – 16); 1% = $\dfrac{3,250}{100}$ = 32.5; 84 × 32.5 = 2,730.

Q21   *Answer* B.

Q22   *Answer* C.
Explanation   To solve such problems, impose a convenient amount as turnover (with percentages, 100 is the ideal arbitrary amount). Charge

reduced by 10% so turnover 100 − 10 = 90. Sales increase by 30% = 130% of 90 = 117. So turnover increases by 17%.

Q23 *Answer* A.

Explanation   The mode is the most frequently occurring value.

Q24 *Answer* B.

Explanation   The median value is the middle value and is identified by arranging the data into numerical order.

Q25 *Answer* C.

Explanation   The lower quartile is found using the equation Q1 = $\frac{1}{4}$ (n + 1)th value.

Q26 *Answer* B.

Explanation   Q3 is found by $\frac{3}{4}$ (n + 1)th value, and the interquartile range is found if you minus Q1 from Q3 = 89 − 27 = 62.

Q27 *Answer* D.

Explanation   The average of any range of consecutive integers must be the average of the smallest and largest numbers from the range. So 282 + 419 = $\frac{701}{2}$ = 350.5.

Q28 *Answer* B.

Explanation $\sqrt{48}$ = 6.92. Prime numbers in the range are 2, 3, 5; 2 and 3 divide exactly into 48, so 48 is not a prime number.

Q29 *Answer* B.

Explanation   Substitute a convenient figure: 100 + (3% of 100) = 103; 103 + (3% of 103) = 106.09.

Q30 *Answer* D.

Explanation   Find the average to find the sum. Calculate the number of items and the average to find the sum. There are 45 numbers (including 16): 60 − 16 + 1 = 45. The average is $\frac{16 + 60}{2}$ = 38.

Sum = average number of items = 38 × 45 = 1,710.

Q31 *Answer* A and C.

Explanation   Try some examples to test it: 3 × 6 = 18, 6 × 6 = 36, 9 × 6 = 54, etc.

Q32 *Answer* A.

Explanation $\dfrac{3 \times 700 + 1 \times 900}{4} = \dfrac{3,000}{4} = 750.$

Q33 *Answer* C.
Explanation $\dfrac{13 + 80}{2} = 46.5$.

Q34 *Answer* B.
Explanation Try some examples: $3 \times 4 = 12$, $3 \times 5 = 15$; $1 + 2 = 3$, $1 + 5 = 6$. Both 3 and 6 are multiples of 3.

Q35 *Answer* B.
Explanation The sum carries over to three digits so the range must begin with 100. The highest value each two-digit number can have is 99 so the highest value in the range must be 198.

Q36 *Answer* D.
Explanation $6 \times 2 \times 70 = 840$. Although the counters are all the same colour, there are still 70 possible outcomes as any one of these could be drawn.

Q37 *Answer* B.
Explanation There are 366 days in a leap year and given that the chance of rain is $\frac{1}{3}$ it would probably rain on 122 of them, but this question is asking about the number of possible outcomes not the probability of the outcome and it is possible that it could rain every day through the year (although this is unlikely).

Q38 *Answer* D.
Explanation They are 678, 786, 876, 687, 867, 768.

Q39 *Answer* A.
Explanation The probability of all possible events must equal 1.

Q40 *Answer* D.
Explanation Mutually exclusive events cannot happen at the same time. An example is tossing a coin where heads and tails are mutually exclusive events.

Q41 *Answer* B.
Explanation In the case of mutually exclusive events the fractions can be added together to get the probability.

Q42 *Answer* A.
Explanation Because the first card is not returned the outcome of the second event is dependent on the outcome of the first. Probability of the second event being a queen (if first not a queen) $= \frac{4}{51}$.

Q43   *Answer* C.
Explanation   Given that there are 4 queens, first event = $^{48}/_{52}$. The second event is slightly more probable, as there are still 4 queens but only 51 cards = $^{47}/_{51}$. So probability that the first two cards are not queens = $^{48}/_{52} \times ^{47}/_{51}$ = 0.9230 × 0.9215 = 0.85 (to two decimal points).

Q44   *Answer* B.
Explanation   For independent events the multiplication rule applies: 0.005 × 0.005 = 0.000025.

Q45   *Answer* B.
Explanation   Probability = $\dfrac{\text{forecast event}}{\text{all possible outcomes}}$.
We know the probability from the previous question and can calculate the number of possible outcomes (assume 365 days a year × 250 possible outcomes a day = 91,250).
$$0.000025 = \frac{x}{91,250}.$$
Forecast event = 2.28125 times (even if the restaurant was open less than every day, B is the most likely answer).

Q46   *Answer* B.
Explanation $^{1,500}/_{6} = 250$.

Q47   *Answer* A.
Explanation   From the previous question we saw that the mean of x is 250 so x minus the mean of x = 150 – 250 = –100.

Q48   *Answer* C.
Explanation   Simply use the x^2 function on a calculator to get the answer.

Q49   *Answer* D.
Explanation   This is simply the sum of column 3.

Q50   *Answer* C.
Explanation $\dfrac{21,250}{6} = 3,541.6$; $\sqrt{3,541.6} = 59.5$.

Test 6: Advanced numeracy test

Q1 *Answer* B.

Explanation An interpolation is an estimate of an unknown number between two known points.

Q2 *Answer* C.

Explanation $5 cm^3 = 125$.

Q3 *Answer* D.

Q4 *Answer* A.

Explanation A reciprocal of a number is found by dividing it into 1.

Q5 *Answer* B.

Explanation $\sqrt{161} = 12.6$. Prime numbers to 12.6 = 2, 3, 5, 7, 11. 7 divides exactly 23 times into 161, so 161 is not a prime number.

Q6 *Answer* A.

Q7 *Answer* B.

Explanation Suggested answer D is a forecasting technique.

Q8 *Answer* A.

Q9 *Answer* A.

Explanation 521 items, average 370. Sum = 521 × 370 = 192,770.

Q10 *Answer* D.

Explanation It would depend on the subject of the population. The number of shirts of all colours and cuts in a store is a finite population. All outcomes in successive rolls of the dice would be infinite.

Q11 *Answer* A.

Explanation $162 + 726 = {}^{888}/_2 = 444$.

Q12 *Answer* A.

Explanation Statistical sampling is a process that makes possible description or the drawing of inferences.

Q13 *Answer* C.

Explanation Simple Pythagorean equation, where $a^2 = c^2 - b^2$:
$a^2 = 8^2 - 3^2 = 55$;
$a = \sqrt{55} = 7.4$.

Q14   *Answer* D.
Explanation   The term is a common one in market research.

Q15   *Answer* D.
Explanation   The difference between quantitative and qualitative research is that the first deals with mathematically measurable items while the second deals with the quality of items.

Q16   *Answer* B.
Explanation   Z will be less than 90%.

Q17   *Answer* B.

Q18   *Answer* C.

Q19   *Answer* C.

Q20   *Answer* D.

Q21   *Answer* C.

Q22   *Answer* D.
Explanation   The original amount = the new amount ÷ (100 + J)/100

Q23   *Answer* E.
Explanation   Statement (1) gives us an absolute value that can describe the advantage Horse A has over Horse B during part of the race. Statement (2) describes a proportional advantage that Horse B has over Horse A during a separate part of the race. Individually neither statement indicates that either horse will complete the course faster than the other. Since an absolute lead cannot be conclusively compared with a proportional lead, the combination of the two statements also gives insufficient information to solve the question.

Q24   *Answer* C.
Explanation   Statement (1) gives us the information required to work out the probability of a ball being drawn by determining the range of possibilities. Statement (2) is necessary as we need to eliminate the possibility that number 7 was one of the first two balls drawn.

Q25   *Answer* A.
Explanation   Statement (1) tells us that the average speed of both aircraft is the same. As we already know that the aircraft cover the same distance we can deduce that the duration of both flights will be the same as time is a function of distance and speed. There is no such relationship

between the weight of the aircraft and the time taken, as other factors such as wind conditions could affect the duration of each flight. This means that statement (2) does not contain sufficient information to answer the question.

Q26   *Answer* C.
Explanation   In this year the minimum wage only increased by 10 pence.

Q27   *Answer* A.
Explanation   The minimum wage has increased from £3.60 to £4.80 over this period – an increase of £1.20. The percentage increase is calculated from $\frac{1.20}{3.60} \times 100$, which rounds to 33%.

Q28   *Answer* D.
Explanation   This is obtained by adding the five values in the second chart.

Q29   *Answer* D.
Explanation   130 + 270 + 440 = 840.

Q30   *Answer* A.
Explanation   Total hotels = 2,300; 23% of 2,300 = 529.

Q31   *Answer* B.
Explanation   529 single beds + 1,081 twins (= 2,162 people) + 437 doubles (= 874 people) + 207 families (= 621) + 46 dormitories (= 184) = 4,370.

Q32   *Answer* B.
Explanation   20% of 47% = 9.4% of 550 3-star hotels = 51.7 × £65 = £3,360.50.

Q33   *Answer* D.
Explanation   (4,001 + 1,219) – (2,552 + 2,156) = 512.

Q34   *Answer* C.
Explanation   (4,001 + 2,552)/(4,001 + 1,219 + 2,552 + 2,156) = 0.66 × 100 = 66%.

Q35   *Answer* D.
Explanation   852 + 102 = $^{954}/_{6,553}$ × 100 = 14.5%.

Q36   *Answer* B.
Explanation   Simply read from the two pie charts. (This is not the greatest sector for either gender.)

Q37   *Answer* C.
Explanation   Each number in the sequence is the sum of the previous number and a number that increments by 1 as the sequence progresses:

10 + 5 = 15;
15 + 6 = 21;
21 + 7 = 28;
28 + 8 = 36;
36 + 9 = 45.

Q38 *Answer* A.

Explanation   Tracing the progression backwards:
10 is the 4th number in the sequence;
10 – 4 = 6 is the 3rd number in the sequence;
6 – 3 = 3 is the 2nd number in the sequence.

Q39 *Answer* B.

Explanation   There is a 5 in 10 chance that the first ball is blue,
which simplifies to a 1 in 2 chance or a probability of 0.5.

Q40 *Answer* D.

Explanation   Be sure you note when the question requires you to calculate
the surface area as distinct from the volume.

Q41 *Answer* A.

Explanation $6 \times 6 \times 6 = 216 \times 3 = 648 \text{cm}^3$.

Q42 *Answer* C.

Q43 *Answer* B.

Q44 *Answer* C.

Explanation $x = {}^{60}/_{10} = 6$.
$s = 6 \times \sqrt{300} = 6 \times 17.3 = 103.8 = 104$.

Q45 *Answer* C.

Explanation   Total reduction = 50 + 10 + 20 = 80%; therefore
£12.50 = 20% of the original price; $^{12.5}/_{20} = 0.625 \times 100 = 62.50$.

Q46 *Answer* D.

Explanation   Number of faces per die = six; two dice, therefore $6 \times 6 = 36$
possible face combinations. There are four possible combinations to get 5:
(1,4), (4,1), (2,3), (3,2); $^4/_{36} = {}^1/_9$.

Q47 *Answer* A.

Explanation   The mode is the answer that is most frequently given – in this
case 3 appears twice whilst all the other answers only appear once.

Q48 *Answer* D.

Explanation Median = 5; mean = $^{66}/_{11}$ = 6; 5 – 6 = –1.

Q49 *Answer* C.

Explanation 400cm × 450cm.

Q50 *Answer* D.

Explanation Volume = $^4/_3\pi r^3$, r^3 = 27, $^4/_3$ × 3.14 × 27 = $\dfrac{4 \times 3.14 \times 27}{3}$ = 113.04.

Test 7: Another advanced numeracy test

Q1 *Answer* C.

Q2 *Answer* A.

Q3 *Answer* C.

Explanation 21 times in the experiments 3 (further 100 times) = 63 times.

Q4 *Answer* A.

Explanation A sphere with a radius of 10cm will have a diameter of 20cm. A cube of 8,000cm³ has sides with a length of 20cm – 20 is the cube root of 8,000 (20 × 20 × 20 = 8,000).

Q5 *Answer* A.

Explanation $\sqrt{113}$ = 10.6. Prime numbers to 10.6 = 2, 3, 4, 7. None divide exactly into 113, so it is a prime number.

Q6 *Answer* B.

Explanation The list is divided into four quarters so the first quartile has three-quarters of the list above it.

Q7 *Answer* B.

Explanation 595 items; average is 393; so sum = 595 × 393 = 233,835.

Q8 *Answer* B.

Explanation This is a list of composite (ie non-prime) whole numbers.

Q9 *Answer* D.

Q10 *Answer* C.

Explanation Arrange the data into numerical order. The median lies between 0 and 1, given that there are eight items.

Q11 *Answer* D.
Explanation No relationship between X and Y is the normal expression of the term 'the null hypothesis'. In practice it means that unless it can be proved otherwise no relationship is assumed.

Q12 *Answer* A.
Explanation $750/(3 + 2) = 150 \times 3 = 450$.

Q13 *Answer* D.

Q14 *Answer* D.

Q15 *Answer* A.

Q16 *Answer* D.

Q17 *Answer* C.
Explanation Subscripts are used to identify items. In mathematics they are below the line. In computing they are in parentheses.

Q18 *Answer* B.
Explanation $^9/_2 = 4.5$; therefore the greatest value of x = 4.

Q19 *Answer* C.

Q20 *Answer* C.

Q21 *Answer* B.
Explanation $1,014 - 696 = 318$.

Q22 *Answer* C.
Explanation $60 - 48 = {}^{12}/_{60} \times 100 = 20\%$.

Q23 *Answer* C.
Explanation $(5,180 + 2,900 + 2,556 + 1,014 + 190) - (2,800 + 1,876 + 1,916 + 696 + 172) = 4,380$.

Q24 *Answer* A.
Explanation $5,180 - 2,800 = {}^{2,380}/_{2,800} \times 100 = 85\%$.
$85\% \times 5,180 = 4,403 + 5,180 = 9,583$.

Q25 *Answer* C.
Explanation The percentage change in 2001 was the lowest, at 3%.

Q26 *Answer* E.
Explanation In 2003 the rate of change in house prices was 12% lower than in 2002.

Q27 *Answer* C.

Explanation   This is obtained by adding the five yearly levels together and dividing this sum by five.

Q28 *Answer* C.

Explanation   A straight trend line should start at around $6\frac{1}{2}$% in 1999, increasing by 3% each year. This line would reach a level of between 20% and 21% if extrapolated to 2004. As this is an estimate, any answer between 17% and 24% would be acceptable.

Q29 *Answer* C.

Explanation $2,412 - 647 = 1,765$.

Q30 *Answer* D.

Explanation $25 + 20 = 45$%.

Q31 *Answer* D.

Explanation $^{734}/_{4,318} \times 100 = 17$%.

Q32 *Answer* B.

Explanation $525 = 15$% of the population; therefore $100\% = {}^{525}/_{15} \times 100 = 3,500$.

Q33 *Answer* A.

Explanation   All the remaining balls must be red, so there is a four in four chance that the seventh ball will be red, which gives a probability of 1.

Q34 *Answer* B.

Q35 *Answer* C.

Explanation   It is a statistical term used to account for unpredicted observations.

Q36 *Answer* A.

Explanation   Imagine looking down on the Earth from the north as it turns, with the Sun's position fixed. If the Earth turns anti-clockwise, any point on the circumference of the Earth will approach the Sun from the east.

Q37 *Answer* C.

Q38 *Answer* B.

Explanation   The standard deviation will be the same as before the wages were increased because the 'spread' or deviation of wages has not changed.

Q39   *Answer* A.

Explanation   Points in a straight line are a perfect correlation but it could be positive or negative, as could any direct correlation.

Q40   *Answer* B.

Explanation $^{10}/_{20} \times {}^{10}/_{20} = {}^{100}/_{400} = {}^1/_4$.

Q41   *Answer* B.

Explanation   The probability is the same as in Q40: $^{10}/_{20} \times {}^{10}/_{20} = {}^{100}/_{400} = {}^1/_4$.

Q42   *Answer* A.

Explanation   The odds always remain the same, as the first sweet is replaced before the next is drawn, so $^1/_4 \times {}^1/_2 = {}^1/_8$.

Q43   *Answer* A.

Explanation $18 \times 5 = {}^{90}/_6 = 15$.

Q44   *Answer* B.

Q45   *Answer* B.

Explanation $102.0 - 100.5 = {}^{1.5}/_{102.0} - 1.5\%$.

Q46   *Answer* D.

Explanation   The probability of the yellow ball being drawn is one in three – which is 33% to the nearest percentage point.

Q47   *Answer* D.

Q48   *Answer* B.

Explanation   The box has 6 sides: 4 sides that are $3 \times 2 = 6$ square metres and 2 sides that are $2 \times 2 = 4$ square metres $= (4 \times 6) + (2 \times 4) = 24 + 8 = 32$ square metres.

Q49   *Answer* C.

Q50   *Answer* D.

Explanation

At start:	100;
After 1 hour:	$100 \times 2 = 200$;
After 2 hours:	$200 \times 2 = 400$; $400 - 50 = 350$;
After 3 hours:	$350 \times 2 = 700$;
After 4 hours:	$700 \times 2 = 1{,}400$; $1{,}400 - 50 = 1{,}350$;
After 5 hours:	$1{,}350 \times 2 = 2{,}700$.

Test 8: Data interpretation

Q1 *Answer* D.

Explanation In 1995 1: 50 or 2 in 100 would be expected to reach age 100 or older. By 2010 this figure has improved to 1:16 or 6.25 in 100. This is an improvement of 4.25 in 100 or 4,250 in 100,000.

Q2 *Answer* B.

Explanation The number of centenarians in 2007 = 9,296 (2008 figure) − 1,000, and 7 women for every man live to age 100 or older. This figure is valid for the last few years and the data set is dated as 2010, so this ratio of 7: 1 can be used for 2008) 8,296 ÷ 8 × 7 = 7,259 women − 1,037 men = 6,222.

Q3 *Answer* A.

Explanation Find 1,000 as a percentage of 8,296. 1% = 82.96, 9,296 ÷ 92.96 = 112.05% so the increase was just over 12%.

Q4 *Answer* C.

Explanation The data set is dated 2010 and the ONS data relating to pensioners is identified as published one month earlier. In 2010 for every child under the age of 16 there are therefore 1.005 pensioners and for every 100,000 children (100,000 × 1.005) there are 100,500 pensioners or 500 more pensioners.

Q5 *Answer* A.

Explanation People in their mid-80s in 1995 will be aged 100 or older in 2010. The number of centenarians in 2008 is given and the rate of annual increase is also stated. The number of centenarians in 2010 can therefore be calculated and the number of people in their mid-80s in 1995 worked out from that. In 2008 there were 9,296 centenarians, so in 2009 there were 9,296 × 105.4% = 9,798 centenarians. The figure for 2010 is 9,798 × 105.4% = 10,327. Multiply this figure by 50 (the number of people in their mid-80s in 1995 who could be expected to live to age 100 or older).

Q6 *Answer* D.

Explanation It is stated that customers in market B perceive the higher price of Morning Tea to imply higher quality. To lower the price therefore risks losing the perception of higher quality and losing sales. It is stated that the buy decision in market A is almost entirely down to price and that the product is sold at a modest premium over competitor brands, so it is reasonable to infer that to remove the premium would result in an increase in sales.

Q7 *Answer* C.

Explanation No year is stated in the question and the magnitude of the difference between the markets varies each year so the best answer is a mean difference over the years. Find this by totalling the values and dividing by the number of years: 479 (market A) ÷ 76 (market B) = 6.3.

Q8 *Answer* B.

Explanation The figures for sales in market A do not support the suggestion that competitor brands are winning Morning Tea's market share and for this reason you should select suggested answer B.

Q9 *Answer* C.

Explanation In 2006 82,400 units were sold for a total value of $120,304 = $1.46 a unit. In 2005 80,000 units were sold for a total value of $120,000 = $1.5 a unit, so the difference is 4 cents.

Q10 *Answer* A.

Explanation The unit value in 2004 = $1.5 (2005 value) × 97% − $1.455. The units sold in 2004 = 58,300 × $1.455 = value of $84,826.5 (add value of market B + 30%) × 130% = $110,274.45.

Q11 *Answer* D.

Explanation there are 2,000 staff and at $150 a delegate all 2,000 staff must have gone on this module to arrive at the total cost of $300,000.

Q12 *Answer* A.

Explanation The average wage = $42,000,000 ÷ 2,000 = 21,000. 21,000 × 5% = 1,050. The training budget divided by the total number of employees = $1,260,000 ÷ 2,000 = $630. $1,050 − $630 = $420.

Q13 *Answer* C.

Explanation $180,500 was spent on the Effective e-mails module at $475 per delegate. 180,500 ÷ 475 = 380. Therefore 380 people attended the module which lasted 1 day, so 380 days were lost.

Q14 *Answer* B.

Explanation The data set states that 60% of staff and associated costs shown relate to staff in sales positions. Therefore the total cost to Training Unlimited for sales staff identified in the data = 60% of the international wage bill plus 60% of the personal development budget = $42,000,000 + $1,260,000 = $43,260,000 × 60% = $25,956,000. Note that it is wrong to calculate the total cost as 105% of $42,000,000 as the total spent on personal development (given in the last table in the data set) is shown as $1,260,000.

Q15 *Answer* D.

Explanation It is stated that 60% of staff and associated costs shown relate to staff in sales positions. It can be calculated that 1,200 staff (60% of all staff) attended the Closing a sale module which is only open to sales staff, but it is not known what percentage of the total staff are in sales positions. Therefore it cannot be calculated what percentage of the total sales staff is represented by the 1,200 staff who attended this module.

Q16 *Answer* C.

Explanation All staff may spend to a maximum of 5% of the average wage on personal development = $1,050. Sales staff may attend the two modules Public speaking and Closing a sale, which total 3 days at a combined cost of £300. They can also attend the Personal safety day at $150, giving a subtotal of 4 days and $450 spent. This leaves $600 of their budget but they can only afford the modules Dealing with conflict or Effective e-mails, both at $475 and lasting 1 day. Therefore the theoretical maximum number of days = 5.

Q17 *Answer* A.

Explanation The total spend on the demonstrating leadership module was $182,000 at a cost of $350 a delegate. $182,000 ÷ $350 = 520, so there were 520 delegates in total, of whom one in four was a woman. 520 ÷ 4 = 130 women. Calculate 130 as a percentage of the total workforce (2,000). 100% = 2,000, 1% = 0.05 × 130 = 6.5%.

Q18 *Answer* D.

Explanation Both a manager and a member of the sales team can attend the Personal safety module ($150) and either Effective e-mails or Dealing with conflict (both of which cost $475). Only a manager can attend the Demonstrating leadership module ($350), and only a member of the sales team can attend Public speaking and Closing a sale ($300). To attend a total of 5 days' training therefore the manager must spend $50 more than a member of the sales team.

Q19 *Answer* B.

Explanation   The budget is set at $1,260,000 and it is clear from the cost table that this was the sum spent. If you selected 60% then you mistakenly calculated the sum of all the personal development values of 2,000 staff at $1,050 a year and found that the spend equalled 60% of this. But this is not the budget.

Q20 *Answer* D.

Explanation   Suggested answer A might appear as if it would save $180,500 at a cost of 380 days' training but it alone would not lead to a cut in the budget because staff could still elect to spend this money by going on other courses. Suggested answer C would fail to secure a cut of 14.3% as $180,000 is $180 less than 14.3% of $1,260,000 and also would not prevent staff from attending other courses.

Q21 *Answer* B.

Explanation   The number of dollar millionaires in 2009 is described as 6% up on the 2008 figure. The 2009 figure of 10,249,988 = 106% of the 2008 figure. Divide 10,249,988 by 106 = 96,698 (= 1%) and multiply by 100 to get the 2008 figure.

Q22 *Answer* C.

Explanation   Find the highest yearly income and subtract the lowest. The highest yearly income is found in Ethiopia = $123 $\times$ 79 million = $9,717,000. The lowest yearly income is earned in Somalia $168 $\times$ 8.5 million = $1,428,000, so the difference is $8,289,000.

Q23 *Answer* D.

Explanation   The per capita income of Mozambique is $81 and of Nepal is $179. Find $179 as a percentage increase on $81. An increase of 221% = 179.01 and is the closest of the suggested answers.

Q24 *Answer* D.

Explanation   The data set states that there are 400,000 dollar millionaires in France but their total net worth is unknown as each may be worth considerably more than a million dollars.

Q25 *Answer* B.

Explanation   There are 8,400,000 dollar a day labourers in Nepal and a total population of 28,000,000. Find 8.4 as a percentage of 28 = 30%.

Q26   *Answer* A.

Explanation   The population in 2007 was 37 million and 4,440 million divided by 37 = $120 per capita income or $35 less than the per capita income in 2009.

Q27   *Answer* D.

Explanation   We have no specific information about the number of Brazilian dollar millionaires. Although we can calculate the number of all new dollar millionaires as 580,198, this is not useful as we are not then able to break the number down by country.

Q28   *Answer* C.

Explanation   In 2009 there were 10,249,998 dollar millionaires and 427,000 of these were from China. Find 427,000 as a fraction of 10,249,998 = approximately $1/_{24}$.

Q29   *Answer* A.

Explanation   Somalia has the highest percentage of dollar a day labourers: 55% (4,675,000 as a percentage of 8,500,000). The next highest percentage is found in Mozambique: 45%.

Q30   *Answer* A.

Explanation   The yearly income in Mozambique in 2009 = 21 $1/_3$ million × $81 = $1,728 million × 5 = $8,640 million ÷ 427,000 (the number of Chinese millionaires) = $20,234.

Test 9: Another data interpretation test

Q1   *Answer* D.

Explanation   In 2008 the population was 305 million. Multiply by 80.8% to find the urban living population and divide by 4 to establish the urban population under 18 years of age = 61.61 million.

Q2   *Answer* B.

Explanation   Of the 305 million population, $1/_4$ are under 18 years of age and $1/_8$ are 65 or more years of age. $1/_4 + 1/_8 = 3/_8$, leaving $5/_8$ of the population aged 18–64 years. 305 million divided by 8 = 38,125,000 × 5 = 190,625,000.

Q3   *Answer* C.

Explanation   The population in 2050 is forecast to be 459,025,000, 40% of whom will be male and 72% of whom will live in states other than Texas or California (100 − 28). 459,025,000 × 40% = 183,610,000 × 72% = 132,199,200.

Q4   *Answer* D.

Explanation   The population was forecast to grow from 305 million to 459.025 million. To find this percentage start with subtraction, 459.025 − 305 = 154.025, then divide 305 by 100 = 3.05 and divide 154.025 by 3.05 = 50.5. The world population is forecast to grow by 37%. 50.5 − 37 = 13.5 or 13.5%.

Q5   *Answer* D.

Explanation   Divide 459.025 by 5.1 to find 1% of world population in 2050 and multiply by 100 to find total world population = 9000.49019607. If world population in 2050 is approximately 9 billion and has grown from 2008 by 37%, to find the 2008 world population: 9 ÷ 137 = 0.0659 × 100 = 6.57007 or 6.570 billion.

Q6   *Answer* A.

Explanation   Output is defined as labour hours, multiplied by units per hour per machine, multiplied by number of machines. The production plant in Bangladesh is plant 2 and team A so the output = 120 × 50 × 15 = 90,000 units. The output for Poland is 144 × 45 × 10 = 64,800. The difference is therefore 25,200.

Q7   *Answer* D.

Explanation   Capital productivity is defined as output divided by the number of machines. Output from the plant in Poland = 144 × 45 × 10 (the number of machines is 10) so capital productivity = 144 × 45 = 6,480. Capital productivity of the plant in Bangladesh = 120 × 50 × 15 (the number of machines is 15) = 6,000, so the difference is 480.

Q8   *Answer* B.

Explanation   Labour productivity is defined as output divided by labour hours. Labour productivity at the plant in Bangladesh is 90,000 ÷ 120 = 750. At the plant in Poland, labour productivity is 64,800 ÷ 144 = 450, so the difference is 300.

Q9   *Answer* D.

Explanation   The information on maximum production is incomplete so you must surmise the most likely significance of the figure given. The maximum production is stated as 810 but it is unclear whether this relates to all machines, each machine, or to one hour, day, week or year of production. It is known that there are 15 machines in the plant. $810 \div 15 = 54$ and this might be a reasonable interpretation of the maximum production of each machine units per hour given that the stated production rate is 50. On this basis the capacity utilization of the plant would be realized when units per hour per machine increased from 50 to 54 and this represents an 8% increase.

Q10   *Answer* D.

Explanation   Mexico's capital productivity (2,760) = output $\div$ 20 (the number of machines at the Mexico plant) so the output of Mexico is 2,760 $\times$ 20 = 55,200. In previous answers the output of Poland was established as 64,800 and Bangladesh 90,000, the mean is found by dividing the sum of these by 3 = 55,200 + 64,800 + 90,000 = 210,000 $\div$ 3 = 70,000.

Q11   *Answer* A.

Explanation   Express the change in jobs in each of the regions as a fraction of the previous total for that region. The region with the second largest relative variation will correspond to the second greatest fraction. South = $^{360,000}/_{2,400,000}$ = $^{36}/_{240}$, South East = $^{270,000}/_{1,600,000}$ = $^{27}/_{160}$ and South West = $^{140,000}/_{2,300,000}$ = $^{14}/_{230}$. Reject the South West region as the smallest, then investigate whether South or South East is the largest. You should be able to see at a glance that the South East fraction $^{27}/_{160}$ is larger than $^{36}/_{240}$ and so the South East region has the largest variation and the South the second largest.

Q12   *Answer* D.

Explanation   The South region has the most jobs under the previous totals and suffered the most job losses. The extent of this loss resulted in the South falling to become the region with the third highest number of jobs (new first is North West, second South West).

Q13   *Answer* B.

Explanation   Previous jobs in the South East region were 1,600,000 and latest jobs are −270,000 giving a new jobs total of 1,330,000. Latest unemployment = 399,000 and this represents 30% of 1,330,000.

Q14   *Answer* C.

Explanation   Only statement C is concerned with the figures alone, whereas the other suggested answers assume some direct relationship between job gains and unemployment. We are provided with no information about the possible relationship between unemployment and the number of jobs, only figures for the level of each. It is clear from the table that jobs increased and unemployment fell but jobs could be filled by newcomers to the labour market (leaving the level of unemployment unaffected), and unemployment might increase in one part of the region and drop in another leaving a modest overall drop. We therefore can only deduce from the data sets that the level of unemployment in the North region dropped relatively little compared to the gain in jobs.

Q15   *Answer* C.

Explanation   The total increase in jobs was 275,000. Of this total, 12% = 33,000 and the region that experienced this increase in jobs is the North region. The new total for jobs in this region is 1,800,000 + 33,000 = 1,833,000.

Q16   *Answer* A, E.

Explanation   Find the means to calculate APS by using the example of the Punjab. APS = average income ÷ average savings APS of population 1 = 8,400 ÷ 1,400 = 6, APS of population 3 = 4. The APS of the Punjab's population is given in the passage as 0.7 and described as among the highest in the world (which means that the lower the APS the higher the propensity to save), so the answer is A, E.

Q17   *Answer* B.

Explanation   The APS of population 2 = 12, population 3 = 4, population 6 = 11, so the population with the lowest APS, ie the population that places the least emphasis on the need to save, is population 3.

Q18   *Answer* C.

Explanation   Find the APS of the three populations by first combining their average income and their average savings to obtain $14,520 (average income) $7,560 (average savings) and then calculate the APS. $14,520 ÷ $7,560 = 1.920, which means that the best estimate from the suggested answers is C.

Q19 *Answer* A, D.

Explanation The current APS of population 6 = 18,700 ÷ 1,700 = 11. This becomes 1,700 + 2,040 = 3,740 (average savings), divide 18,700 by 3,740 = 5. The propensity has improved by 6 (11 – 5 = 6). So the answer is A, D.

Q20 *Answer* C.

Explanation Calculate the current APS = 4, then find the new APS given the new average income = $39,750/4 = $9,937.5 (the new level of saving if APS does not change). Now minus the original average savings to find by how much average saving would need to increase: $9,937.5 – $7,950 = $1,987.5.

Q21 *Answer* D.

Explanation The target for 2007 is $72,000 which if missed by 15% = ($72,000 × 85%) = $61,200 + revenue for 2006 ($2,400,000) = $2,461,200.

Q22 *Answer* A.

Explanation The revenue for 2007 = total revenue 2006 plus targets for 2007 = $7,400,000 (total revenue 2006) + $134,750 (total of targets 2007) = $7,534,750.

Q23 *Answer* B.

Explanation The revenue growth target for 2008 = 2.5% while in $ terms the target for 2007 = $6,500 expressed as a percentage of $1,300,000. 1% = $13,000 so $6,500 = 0.5% or in percentage terms 2% less than the 2008 target.

Q24 *Answer* A.

Explanation The combined revenue growth target for 2007 is $5,250 + $27,000 = $32,250, and the combined 2006 revenue was $700,000 + $1,800,000 = $2,500,000. Expressed as a percentage of 2006 revenue the revenue growth target = $2,500,000 ÷ 100 = 1% = $25,000. Divide 32,250 by 25,000 = 1.29 or 1.29%.

Q25 *Answer* D.

Explanation With sources 1 and 4 it would be possible to estimate the size of the confectionery market. Sources 2, 3 and 4 would provide insight into the character of the distributors of confectionery and competitors' market share rather than the potential market.

Q26 *Answer* B.

Explanation Revenue in 2007 will be $3,500 below target and in 2008 will be $3,500 × 101% below target = $3,535. Add these two sums to calculate the total revenue shortfall. $3,500 + $3,535 = $7,035.

Q27 *Answer* C.

Explanation Suggested answers A and B would least support the achievement of the target growth in revenue. Answer C is preferable over D because it would provide a more effective assessment of marketing activities (both C and D would support the achievement of revenue growth targets).

Q28 *Answer* A.

Explanation In 2006 revenue = $1,300,000. For 2007 = £1,300,000 + ($6,500 × 20) $130,000 = $1,430,000. Revenue for the two years combined = $2,730,000.

Q29 *Answer* C.

Explanation The 2007 revenue growth target calculated as a percentage of its 2006 revenue for Hard Gums is 0.5%, so you must find the product with a revenue growth target calculated as a percentage of its 2006 revenue of 3% (6 times greater). This is Cool Mints ($72,000 as a percentage of $2,400,000 = 3%).

Q30 *Answer* B.

Explanation Statement 4: 'The figures for Fruit Salad in 2007 and 2008 combined give a target revenue increase of 3%' is not valid. The increase in 2007 for Fruit Salad is $24,000 on $1,200,000 which is 2%. Add this to the percentage target for 2008 (2%) and it is clear that the statement is not valid). All the other suggested answers are valid.

Interpretations of your test scores

Test 1: Key quantitative operations

A score above 60

If you face one of the higher-level psychometric tests such as GMAT, Fast Stream or SHL Graduate Battery, this is the only category of score that you should be content with. To excel in these tests you must be able to demonstrate speed, accuracy, confidence and familiarity with these basic operations and your score suggests that you did exactly this, so you have made a good start!

Go on to the tests and practices contained in the latter sections and be confident that you are adopting the right approach to ensure that you perform well in the demanding psychometric tests used by employers and educational institutions.

A score of 50 or above

Establish which principles were involved in the questions that you got wrong and start a programme of practice that begins with the revision of these operations. Once you have become confident in these and all the key operations reviewed in this test, move on to the further material covered by this title.

If you found that you did not have enough time to complete all the questions, practise estimating the answers rather than working the whole sum, look to rule out some suggested answers as wrong and thereby narrow the field of possible answers. Practise more, with a view to increasing your confidence and speed.

You will find additional suitable material in my book *How to Pass Advanced Numeracy Tests* (Kogan Page, 2008).

A score below 50

To compete with the best consider setting aside a quite significant amount of time to review the key skills examined by advanced numeracy tests. With practice you will succeed in acquiring the confidence, accuracy and speed in answering these questions. It may take time, it might even be painful – you may have to work hard at revising long-forgotten rules and rusty mental arithmetic – but if the opportunity to which you are working is something you really want, then go for it. You have nothing to lose. Follow the advice in the early sections on how to organize your programme of practice. Track down sufficient material on which to work. Get started in plenty of time and begin with the key operations covered in this section. When you have realized confidence, speed and accuracy in the operation of these concepts, move on to the material covered in the remaining sections of this book. You will find lots of suitable material in the books listed on page 3.

Test 2: Fundamental accounting terms

A score above 27

If you face the ABLE Financial Appraisal Exercise, this is the only score you should be content with. Your score suggests a high level of confidence and familiarity with the fundamental vocabulary of accounting and business. This language is taken for granted in the workplace and a command of it is assumed in many advanced numeracy tests. You can expect to perform well in this aspect of these tests and so should concentrate on other challenges in order that you perform to this high standard in all spheres.

A score of 20 or above

You realized a good score but if you face one of the highly competitive tests for a senior managerial position then you should seek to further enhance your confidence and command of these fundamental terms. Achieve this by reading more of the specialist business journals, check the definitions of any terms with which you are not familiar and practise the language of business at every opportunity.

A score below 20

The language examined by this test is fundamental to the day-to-day operation of every business, and a working knowledge of it is expected in both the workplace and the psychometric tests used to recruit to that work place. To succeed in the competitive tests used by employers you need to develop greater confidence in using, and a command of, this language. You will realize this through, for example, reading the business section of a quality newspaper and the weekly specialist business journals. Obtain a dictionary of business terms and look up any words that you do not understand.

Test 3: Business comprehension

A score above 85

This test was not only an examination of your command of the language of business but also a test of your endurance and ability to stay focused. Your score suggests that you demonstrate all these qualities. Concentrate your remaining practice on other challenges confident in the knowledge that you have a command of the terminology of business that will serve you well.

A score of 65 or above

This is a good score but if you face one of the highly competitive tests for a senior managerial position, you should seek to further enhance your confidence and command of these fundamental terms. It may be that you simply could not answer all the questions in the given time or that you found it difficult to work at the same rate right up to the end. If this was the case, read more of the specialist business journals, check the definitions of any terms with which you are not familiar and practise building up your levels of concentration and focus by taking more practice tests. Remember that to do well in these tests you really have to work very hard.

A score below 65

The language examined by this test is typical of that used in the business press and workplace, and a working knowledge of it is expected in the psychometric tests of advanced numeracy.

Seek to develop greater confidence in using this language by reading the business section of a quality newspaper and the weekly specialist business journals. Obtain a dictionary of business terms and look up any words that you do not understand.

Test 4: A test of geometry

A score above 40

Not every advance numeracy test includes questions of geometry. However, GMAT does and if you face this test your score suggests that you will excel in this aspect of it. As you can expect to perform well in this aspect of the test you face, you can concentrate on other challenges in order that you perform to this high standard across the board.

A score of 30 or above

It is a good result but it could be better! Not every advance numeracy test includes geometry questions but a number do and if you face one of these you should under-take some more practice and ensure that you pick up all of these marks rather than most of them. Go over your result and see if there are any rules or formulae that you can memorize. If you ran out of time, practise more so that you build up your speed and confidence. It may be that you have to take more risks in terms of risking getting some questions wrong in order to attempt more questions. You have to achieve a difficult balance between speed and accuracy where you manage all the questions in the time given but minimize errors because you are rushing. Only practice will help achieve this balance.

A score below 30

It may be that the test you face does not include questions of geometry. Establish for sure whether or not it does. If the answer is no, forget triangles and cosine ratios and practise on the questions that are directly relevant to the challenge ahead. If the test you face does indeed involve geometry questions, these represent relatively straight-forward marks, and with more practice you can guarantee these points count towards your overall score. Revise and memorize the rules and formulae. Many are covered in the chapter 'A key concepts reference' and the explanations offered with the answers. Learn the sequence of square and cube numbers. Then practise until you get the questions right every time. Finally practise under realistic test conditions.

Test 5: A further test of quantitative operations

A score above 40

Your score suggests a high level of confidence and familiarity in these operations. You can expect to perform well in a real test of these concepts and so you can concentrate on other challenges in order that you perform to this high standard every time.

A score of 30 or above

Establish which principles were involved in the questions that you got wrong and start a programme of practice that begins with the revision of these operations. Once you have become confident in these and all the key operations reviewed in this test, practise on further mock tests under realistic test conditions – if you do this I am confident that you will notice a significant improvement in your score.

If you found that you did not have enough time to complete all the questions, practise estimating the answers rather than working the whole sum. Look to rule out some suggested answers as wrong and thereby narrow the field of possible answers. Practise more with a view to increasing your confidence and speed.

You will find suitable material in my book *How to Pass Advanced Numeracy Tests* (Kogan Page, 2008). Other sources are also listed on page 3 of this book.

A score below 30

To compete, set aside a quite significant amount of time to review the further operations examined in this test. With practice you will succeed in acquiring the confidence, accuracy and speed in answering these questions. It may take time, but if the opportunity to which you are working is something you really want then go for it. Follow the advice in the early sections on how to organize your programme of practice. Track down sufficient material on which to work and get started in plenty of time.

Tests 6 and 7: Advanced numeracy

A score above 40

If you face one of the higher-level psychometric tests such as GMAT or Fast Stream, this is the only category of score that you should be content with. To excel in these tests you must be able to demonstrate speed, accuracy, confidence and familiarity with all these principle operations and your score suggests that you have done exactly this, so well done!

A score of 30 or above

You did well but you can do better so don't settle until you have achieved an even better score. Keep improving your mental arithmetic, continue revising the funda-mental sequences, then you can recognize, without doing the calculation, the correct answers to many questions. Make sure that you are confident in the operation of all the key operations. Practise to maintain your focus and to develop a test technique then ensure that you attempt every question in the time allowed. Remember that to do well in these tests you have to try really hard and attend on the day fully prepared.

A score below 30

Go over your answers identifying each type of question that you got wrong. Use the explanation provided to better understand the demands of the question. Seek out further examples of these questions and practise at them until you master them. Don't give up; just keep practising at getting right these key operations and building up your speed and confidence.

Tests 8 and 9: Data interpretation

A score above 25

If you face one of the higher-level psychometric tests such as the SHL Graduate Battery or the ABLE Financial Assessment, this is the only category of score that you should be content with. To excel in these tests you must be able to demonstrate speed, accuracy, confidence and familiarity with all these principle operations and your score suggests that you have done exactly this, so well done!

A score of 20 or above

You did well but you can do better so don't settle until you have achieved an even better score. Keep improving your mental arithmetic and continue revising the fundamental sequences, then you can recognize, without doing the calculation, the correct answer to many questions. Make sure that you are confident in the operation of all the key operations. Practise to maintain your focus and to develop a test technique then ensure that you attempt every question in the time allowed. Remember that to do well in these tests you have to try really hard and attend on the day fully prepared.

A score below 20

Go over your answers identifying each type of question that you got wrong. Use the explanation provided to better understand the demands of the question. Seek out further examples of these questions and practise them until you master them. Don't give up; just keep practising at getting right these key operations and building up your speed and confidence.